T

MW01171953

The American Exposé

Apostasy in the Church

DR. JUNE DAWN KNIGHT

TreeHouse Publishers

The American Exposé

@2020 Dr. June Dawn Knight

3rd Edition, #5 in the *We are the Bride Series*

1st Book in the **American Quad**

For more information about the author go to:

www.drjune.org

www.wearethebride.us

www.watbradio.com

www.watb.tv

TreeHouse Publishers
Dreams Come True in Our House!

TreeHouse Publishers
www.gotreehouse.org
Printed in the United States of America

DEDICATION

I dedicate this book to my mother, Wilma June Bracey. She passed away on 01/22/17. I feel like she is a part of this because she passed away halfway through my 40-Day Fasting & Praying initiative with the team for President Trump and the nation. Following this adventure and her death is when God launched me nationwide.

My mother has always been a strong woman. I could not do this without the leading she gave me as a mother. She taught me to be strong and now I'm thankful. I miss her so much!

Now that God has revealed what is coming to our country, I'm very thankful the Lord took her home. She already suffered enough with her failing health. I'm so thankful she's healed now! I love you mom!

Wilma JJ Carpenter Bracey
02/17/1941 - 1/22/2017

INTRODUCTION

Hello Bride. I call you Bride because my ministry is "We are the Bride (WATB) Ministries". The Lord gave me a vision years ago that I am a protector/guardian of the Bride. I am serving you like the Levites did to the Children of Israel. He told me, "You take care of her and she will take care of you." So, you will see in my writings that I am basically defending our faith against the enemy. I am looking out for you and therefore you will see me give advice, what to look out for, etc. It's because I see myself as your mom. The Lord blessed me in bible college in 2005 with the motherly anointing from Mama Parsley. So, now when you read my books you can understand the slant I'm writing from.

In these books, my heart is really grieved over what is happening in our country. I do not take it lightly what I'm implicating. I have cried about this to the Lord time and time again because I realize that most of you reading this book are in the apostasy and do not even realize it. You really love the Lord and are just trying so hard to please Him. This is how I was when I discovered that I was in it too. Now that it's been revealed by the Holy Spirit, I hope to educate you and teach about what I've learned. I am trying to empower you Bride to finish your course. You know the Bible says that we will perish due to lack of knowledge. So, we must be good stewards of the word.

As well, when you see names in this book of people and ministries, businesses, etc., who are involved in all this mess; please know it grieves me to expose this.

However, the Lord has directed me to be very frank and upright with you Bride. I must be plain about it because everyone else is being politically correct and beating around the bush with the truth. I cannot do that.

I must tell you the exact truth and allow you to go back to God and pray about it. Ask him to confirm and show you. These books may be just that confirmation you needed. Either way, it's very important that we read these books with a prayer asking God to take that religious spirit from us so that we can see the big picture.

The time has come Bride that we all heard about when we were children. The hour of the fulfillment of the Book of Revelation. The end of days is here and what an amazing time to be alive!

Through my years of research into the mark of the beast, etc., and my current research into the discovery of why the church is sick, I have discovered the great apostasy is upon us! We are now in the great deception! The Lord took me to London in grad school in 2012 to show me the worldly plans of the mark of the beast, then seven (7) years later he brought me all the way to the White House to see it being implemented. **The beast system is being put together now while we are being distracted by the mainstream media with all the drama in Washington DC.**

****WARNING! WARNING!** – This book will probably shock you and may even devastate you because of your own participation in this and NOT KNOWING the big picture. I pray you seek the Lord and do not fall back or retreat. God is revealing this to you so that you can be set free and be prepared for the judgment and the hour of visitation on the Earth. PLEASE READ ALL OF IT TO GAIN FULL UNDERSTANDING AND TRUTH.****

This all began when I completed the 40 Days Fasting & Prayer Initiative from January 1 to February 10, 2017. Each day I prayed with a team of people for President-elect Donald J. Trump.

We also prayed for his cabinet, the country, families, the church/Bride and any other thing the Holy Ghost highlighted.

This was an intense prayer time and included my mother passing away halfway through it on January 22nd. She was so happy to see President Trump win.

During this time of consecration, the Lord moved mightily! Following this event is when the Lord took me across the country on the *Making America Godly Again (MAGA) March for Revival* tour.

I went on that tour believing that America will be so happy to march declaring that Jesus is Lord over our nation and we are a Christian nation again. However, when I left for the trip it didn't take me long to realize something was wrong. There was great anger in the country about Donald Trump as our new president. I was shocked to learn that it was very evident even in the church; and mostly from the African-American community.

I did not realize how bad it was until I hit the road and began talking to people all over the country. I will write more about this later in the book.

Also, up until this trip, I was involved with many ministries across the country and didn't realize the full impact of what I was looking at. I just knew that all we ever talked about was the great revival coming. When I did the MAGA Revival Tour, it was only appropriate because it was paving the way for the big one!

After about ¼ of the trip I arrived in Houston. I received a word from the Lord that informed me that the Lord had a different purpose for me on this trip and it was to show me the sickness in the church. He said that He had me "hidden" during this process. I had already begun to see things on the road that are troubling, but after that word, I saw with great clarity.

Completing the six-month tour, I prayed and inquired of the Lord about what to do with this information.

It is so sad it grieves your heart. It grieved me for a while to where I just wanted to quit and not tackle this beast. When I saw that 90% of the church is in a great deception, I really struggled because I did not want to be labeled for the rest of my life. I've known for years that I was a watchman on the wall but did not want to go down that road because it seems so negative and against the flow. It's easier just doing interviews and meeting people. It's easier on the flesh because it is fun and exciting.

However, after traveling I realize that the Bride is sick. She has been overtaken by a virus and I am hoping to partner with Heaven to bring awareness to what I've discovered about the pollution in the waters of the church. I can see that she is tainted and is not aware of the darkness that has crept in. However, the challenge becomes on what do I do with this information? Should I stand up in the midst of the beast and yell from the mountaintops or sit down and do nothing. After all, I am a woman and according to their standards am not wealthy; thus not successful. I live completely by faith. Who am I?

I began producing *The Clarion Call* TV show to show the symptoms of what I was seeing. Man, I could not even imagine the persecution! Immediately I lost over 350 followers! I'm talking ministers! When I began exposing New Age things that we brought in the church and our homes, along with the tattoos, I began to see a great exodus. I had ministers calling me names, putting me down, yelling at me, etc. I wrote a post and told all those prideful men (pastors/leaders) that I was not the kind of woman they could threaten. I'm not backing down. After that they backed off.

It wasn't until I began researching these symptoms did I learn about the true root of the virus.

This book will expose that root, so the Bride can be set free!

Then the Lord gave me a dream in November of 2017 and told me to do 40 days of prayer again on January 1, 2018 and cast down one idol a day. These idols are what the church has raised up before His nostrils. We fasted and prayed for 40 days and those idols are included in the 2nd book. You will see how most of the characteristics we had to repent about are from this virus.

This is the great apostasy and deception. I hope people get delivered.

The spiritual warfare has been ramped up against the church and this book will expose one of the biggest tactics that the enemy is using against us. He wants to blind and distract God's people so that they do not make it until the end. He wants her to give up and throw in the towel or worship him without being detected. He comes as an angel of light to deceive and in this book, I am blowing the lid off this heresy and exposing the enemy!

Bride, I do not take it lightly who will be reading this book. You are chosen by God to be used in the last few moments of time to help others to see the truth.

The Bible says to expose the darkness! (Eph. 5:11) Truth is the most important thing right now because the deception is so thick. How do we measure truth? By the word of God! The Spirit of God is not going to contradict the Bible. They work together. They should confirm one another.

From the White House to the average houses, the deception is thick and deep. I pray this book opens your eyes to the truth. You are chosen for such a time as this.

This book is the **1st book in the American Quad**. It will identify the sickness in the church that God revealed to me in the *MAGA Revival Tour* trip in **2017**. This book identifies the problem (apostasy).

The 2nd book, The American Idols, exposes the 40 idols that God brought before the 40-Day Team to address the throne. This team repented to God in the first 40 days of **2018**. Once the church gets real with God, we can find true repentance. Unless you recognize the sickness, you cannot fix it.

The 3rd book, The American Judgment, exposes the resulting judgment that is coming to the church due to the non-repentant church and nation. This was revealed fully in **2019** when God put me in Washington DC to warn the President, Republican Party and the country of the dangers of partnering with LGBTQ. This book examines the Biblical standpoint on judgment and the church's role today.

The 4th book is The Last American Bride. Where do we go from here and how do we prepare for the future? Now we are in **2020**. New decade, new destiny. What about the mark of the beast? What about technology? False prophets in the church, etc. Martyrdom? All four books are the prepare the Bride for the days ahead. Persecution is coming. It will cover what the TRUE church looks like, and how you can get INVOLVED and BE the solution to the problems. We will examine the different false teachings and provide precisely what the truth is and practical things you can do to live out the truths. Prepare for the ending we were designed for!

CONTENTS

Dr. June Dawn Knight

1

Royal Moment of Time

Time is a gift that God grants each human. In His reality, time is not a factor. However, in our reality, it is everything. If we waste it, we can never recover it. The Lord revealed to me many years ago how precious time is for us as humans.

Five years ago, the Lord took me on a journey of praying with people on their death beds for a year and a half. During this time, I met so many ages and types of people. I saw many scenarios of death. Although I was afraid of what to say to these precious people, the Lord was always with me to fill my mouth with the right words. He is so amazing!

I can promise you that when your time comes to leave this Earth, you will not be laying there wondering if you had a better career or bigger house or more money. No, you will be wondering two things. Where is my family and am I ready to die? This is where I stepped in. I assisted them to know and be ready.

If you read my previous books, you heard me tell the story of a man named Benjamin. He was 101 years old and I prayed with him on his deathbed in 2013. He was in a coma and when I laid hands on him I was catapulted into heaven with him.

I saw how the heavenly host greeted him. They treated him like he was royalty! About a month later, the Lord gave me a song in a dream called ROYAL MOMENT OF TIME.

This song proclaimed how he served his church for 75 years, married to his wife for 73, served five pastors, and held no position but servanthood the whole time! The Lord showed me how this man led a humble life, and, in the end, it paid off! He got his just reward! It was beautiful!

Why Are We Here On Earth

I read the whole Book of Revelation the other day to make sure again that I understand what is coming before I release this book. Did you know that God has a temple in Heaven? Yes! He has a temple! In Heaven we are known as his servants. (Rev. 2:20) Yes, we are the sons and daughters of God, but we are also servants. We are here on the Earth to serve God. It's all about mission and revealing who God is on the Earth as we learn more about him and who we are IN HIM. When we stand before God on judgment day, we will be held accountable to what we did with that time that he granted us. (2 Cor. 5:10) Did we waste it, or did we obey him and allow him to do what He needed to for the Kingdom as a whole? This is a hard concept to grasp on this Earth because the world tells us differently. The world tells us to live for me, myself, and I. Think of yourself only. This is not the way in the kingdom of God. He wants us to serve Him as His servants and to turn around and serve others as well.

Think about how Jesus taught his disciples to be a servant. He taught them to serve others by washing their feet and to prefer others above themselves.

Why does God require us to have a servant's heart? He requires it because He has given so much to us freely. Freely you have received, freely give.

2

He wants us to help others on this journey of life and give to them selflessly. See, the Tree of Life is selfless.

We are here for a specific reason Bride. God chose you to be the last bride! What an honor! Your destiny is to reveal another aspect of who God is. Your life is to reveal a certain aspect of his glory. You were chosen before time began!

Think about it Bride. Think about the Bride that is about to go through the Great Tribulation! We will be the ones to stand up to the Beast and tell him NO! We will NOT take that mark/chip! So, many of us will die through martyrdom because of it. This is an honor! Then the ones that survive will be raptured up around the half-way point in Tribulation. At that point, we will all stand before the throne on that sea of glass! I talk about all of this in *The American Judgment* book.

However, you are chosen to be the ones wearing the white robe and standing before the throne as overcomers! Then, we will experience the Marriage Supper of the Lamb! Then we will be the ones coming back on the horses with Jesus on his white horse and we will split the sky wide open! We will come back for the Battle of Armageddon! We will defeat Satan's army. Then we will rule and reign as kings and priests during the Millennial Reign! For 1,000 years we can experience Jesus' kingdom! This is THE REAL KINGDOM OF GOD!

So, you were chosen to be the generation that will officially end the time of humans and then celebrate throughout eternity. HOWEVER, you will have a battle on your hands to finish this race! That's what this book is for! I am equipping you with truth! The last book in this series, *The Last American* Bride, is a resource book to help the last Bride to be equipped with knowledge about the enemy's plans. It is an equipping book. This will help.

The Tree of Life Represents Truth & God

God describes the Tree of Life in many places. In the beginning it is in the Garden of Eden. This tree was in the garden and Adam and Eve could eat of it freely. However, they chose the wrong tree. At the end of the Bible it's in the Great Millennium. During this time, we have 12 different kinds of fruit and we will eat it for the healing of the nations. (Rev. 22). This tree is from heaven and this is the one that we pull from.

> **Revelation 22:14 Blessed are they that do his commandments, that they may have right to the tree of life, and may enter in through the gates into the city.**

The Tree of Life is still available to us today. This is Jesus. He is the vine. When we stay attached to this tree and eat the fruits on it, we will be successful!

The Tree of Knowledge of Good and Evil

Represents Compromise & Twisting of the Truth

The Tree of Knowledge of Good and Evil is all about self. It's very selfish. This tree puffs up. Think of what it did to Eve. First, it twisted the truth. It took a little bit of false and mixed it in with the truth. Consider Satanism's greatest commandment, "Do as thou wilt." Check this out, "Our position is to be self-centered, with ourselves being the most important person (the "God") of our subjective universe, so we are sometimes said to worship ourselves." (Church of Satan, 2020)

> *Genesis 2:16-17 - 16 And the Lord God commanded the man, saying, Of every tree of the garden thou mayest freely eat:17 But of the tree of the knowledge of good and evil, thou shalt not eat of it: for in the day that thou eatest thereof thou shalt surely die.*

This is how God instructed him in the beginning. Now look and see how Satan twisted what God said:

> *Genesis 3:1-5 - 1 Now the serpent was more subtle than any beast of the field which the Lord God had made. And he said unto the woman, Yea, hath God said, Ye shall not eat of every tree of the garden? 2 And the woman said unto the serpent, We may eat of the fruit of the trees of the garden: 3 But of the fruit of the tree which is in the midst of the garden, God hath said, Ye shall not eat of it, neither shall ye touch it, lest ye die. 4 And the serpent said unto the woman, Ye shall not surely die, 5 For God doth know that in the day ye eat thereof, then your eyes shall be opened, and ye shall be as gods, knowing good and evil.*

Notice how Satan twisted God's command. "Ye shall not surely die, For God doth know that in the day ye eat thereof, then your eyes shall be opened, and ye shall be as gods, knowing good and evil." (vs. 4 & 5). See how he twisted the simple command of "Of every tree of the garden thou mayest freely eat: But of the tree of the knowledge of good and evil, thou shalt not eat of it: for in the day that thou eatest thereof thou shalt surely die." (vs. 16 & 17).

Satan not only twisted what God said, but he added to the command of simply "do not eat". He added the commentary that "the reason God does not want you to do this is because HE KNOWS.....".

It's very accusatory towards God like God is holding them back from being all that He wants them to be because they are limited in their knowledge.

Satan is still up to his same 'ole tricks. These groups, Ecumenical Movement, Emergent Church, and New Apostolic Reformation; this is what they seek after. They are steeped in mysticism.

They seek after more than the limits that God restrains them to.

NAR teaches obedience a lot. It's just false in the sense that it's obedience to the revelation from experiences more than obedience to the Word of God. They are then adding to the word of God and making a tradition of men (ideas/teachings from these experiences) more important and exciting than the literal Word of God. We will talk about this later.

One other thing I want to point out about eating from this wicked tree. The fruit tastes GOOD. It is delicious when we are sinning, and our flesh is satisfied. When we walk a Christian life, we must deny our flesh. Although it tastes good…we must resist.

The Apostasy is Robbing Our Time

The apostate church has changed the doctrine over the past 30-40 years and twisting the ending story. This deceives the church into thinking they have more time. What are the lies that the NAR and other false prophets have spun in their evil web?

- Some teach that Jesus is coming in a pre-trib rapture. This is a new doctrine that began in the 1700s and spread through the *Scofield Bible.* It's a relatively new doctrine but cannot be backed up scripturally. So, when the mark of the beast is being implemented, etc., this group can say, "Go ahead and take the mark because the rapture hasn't happened yet." Then this will send millions of Christians to Hell. This doctrine is contradicted in Matthew 24.

- Others say that Jesus already came back in 70AD (preterist), and now all we expect is for Him to return and set up his 1,000 year kingdom on the Earth in Jerusalem. This is why they have partnered with the Jews and Israel. (Zionists). This group also backed off winning people to Jesus (conversion) because they now believe that the Jews are not bound by Jesus' commandment of him being the only way to God the Father in salvation. They believe that the Jews can get to Heaven by the first covenant. This is why you see Christian/Jewish combined conferences without pleading for the church to win the lost Jews before Jesus returns! It's very sad.

- They also teach that all faiths will return to Jerusalem, build the temple and become AS ONE. They teach that all will be in unity and this is the great revival they are pushing for now. They have partnered all religions without telling the evangelicals that they have done this. They are being very sneaky. We will talk more about this.

In other words, you must ask your pastor or group leaders what do they believe about eschatology, or end of times. This is key to your spiritual health. If they are in this group that does not believe that the Antichrist is about to be revealed and the one world order is being put in place, then you are in a dangerous place.

This IS the apostasy. They have blinded the church and lulled them into sleep while the Beast is making way. They have kept the country distracted through the Washington DC fighting and President Trump's Tweets and impeachment facade.

Time is Up: Our Time Has Come

Many people question whether we are at the end of times or do we have more time. The answer that we must settle in our hearts now is that our time is up. This is it. The Book of Revelation has escalated and now we are about to step into Tribulation. If you are reading this book during Tribulation, then know that I'm finishing this book in early 2020. We may have a few years to prepare for what's coming, however, I believe we are right at the door of entering the seven (7) year Tribulation. According to biblical prophecy, we are at the crest of stepping into the Tribulation period.

We have fulfilled all the signs to this point in prophecy. What this means to us as his final Bride is that we are stepping into the most trying and cataclysmic point in history. We are stepping into an era that many have feared throughout that last 2,000 years. When you think about it, we're very blessed that God chose us. This could have been anyone else. However, He chose you and me. He knows we can do this. We are built, tried, tested, purified and created for this moment we are stepping into. We do not need to fear because God is with us.

I DO WANT TO CLARIFY THAT I'M NOT SETTING DATES, BUT RATHER I AM SOUNDING THE ALARM THAT TIME IS UP. IT MAY BE A WEEK, MONTH, YEAR OR A FEW YEARS, BUT NO MATTER HOW MUCH TIME IS LEFT…THIS IS IT!

As I studied the Old Testament from Genesis to Deuteronomy, and Ezekiel, I realize how God was with all those leaders through their judgments. In my book – *The American Judgment*, I examine God's pattern of judgment and current day situation.

For instance, with Moses I am amazed how God spoke to him and instructed him on almost every move to make! In addition, God gave him a stick (rod) to use and display the supernatural powers.

Whenever God performed something out of Moses, he had to hold his stick over his head. For instance, when he parted the Red Sea, he held his rod up! When they were in battle, he held it high. It's beautiful reading how Aaron helped him when his arm got weak. Then let's consider Joseph. This story is so amazing because God was right there with him through it all! This story filled me with so much hope because God was with him in his pit, in prison, and everywhere!

I realized after reading all those stories why God was so adamant on them not having a king. He was so close to them and wanted to be their king. He was jealous of them. He wanted them seeking Him for everything.

When the Children of Israel wanted a king this hurt God's heart so much because it made him feel like he wasn't good enough to lead them. They wanted their Egyptian ways so much that they did not want to do it His way. So, He ended up giving them what they wanted. However, as time went on we saw how the power went to the king's heads and they wouldn't listen to God.

See how the power shifted from God talking through the prophets and them being living examples to the people? Now it's kings who are way above the people. When you think about it, this is the exaggerated prosperity gospel today. We wanted money and power so much that we created this kingdom of the rich rulers over us.

One man on a platform and everyone else throwing money at him declaring blessings over those that give 10,000 dollars or more. "Send me $10,000 and you receive a special word from me."

People, this is spiritual whoredom to God. This is a vomit in His mouth. Gross! God would never do this.

It's not examining our hearts anymore but a superficial aspect of worldly security financially. See how the Children of Israel were so satisfied with their captivity because their needs were met. I mean think about it Bride; If the ministers involved in this prosperity movement had that much prosperity, why would they need to manipulate the Bride? Why manipulate, sell and swindle things to get financing for the kingdom? Think about it! Where is their faith? (prosperity ministers today). I do know of some ministers who never manipulate the Bride for money and God always supplies it.

Our Christianity has been tainted with this, and now if we have a disaster in our country and those people get challenged without money or lose their material things, what will do they do when their "blessings" are gone? Where will their faith be? They sold out their birthright for finances and security. This is how that doctrine is to us spiritually. We sell out our real inheritance from God desiring (or lusting) after material things. Manipulation is as the sin of Witchcraft. 1 Sam 15:23

In this book, I will give you terms and definitions so that you can understand it. Most of this I learned through research. I learned a lot more when I served in the White House as a correspondent for a year. I sat in many governmental meetings, received their information, God blessed me behind the scenes to be in high-level prayer meetings, etc. God took me to the top to show me what I'm writing to you about in these books.

I encourage you not to quickly dismiss these books. The Devil has stolen enough time from you. We want to maximize the time we have left to full potential for God! The Devil is a liar!

Let's Say a Prayer

In addition to what you're about to read, I want you to take a moment now to pray this:

Holy Spirit, I ask you to help me to understand what I'm about to read. Help me to have eyes to see and ears to hear from you. I want to be equipped for this last mission. I want to know what I am and what I'm called to do in this hour. I can't do this without you and I need you. You're my teacher and my guide. Thank you. In the name of Jesus, amen.

Well Bride, time is out, and we must examine our hearts while we still have time. We must clean out our closets and allow God to reveal to us what we need to remove and deal with so that we can be used by Him in this epic moment we're stepping into. Here's a prayer to help you with this:

God, I love you so much. I just want to thank you for allowing me to live for such a time as this. I know that you created me for this moment and you know I can do all things as long as you're with me. I want to be used at maximum potential with nothing holding me back. So, I need you Lord to examine my heart. Your word says that the Holy Spirit is the searcher of man's hearts so I'm asking you Holy Spirit to search deep within my heart right now. Search me Lord! Bring it to the surface any roots of bitterness I may have. Please let me know if there is any unforgiveness in my heart. Reveal to me my own heart. Lord please help me to overcome myself. I can't do this without you. I trust in you Lord. In Jesus' name. Amen

Note of Encouragement about Time

I know Bride that this is not easy. It's hard facing yourself! It is necessary because time has gotten away from us and we must regain the time while we still can. THE TIME HAS COME TO ACT!

I understand the battle of facing yourself before a holy God. One time I was in bible college in the middle of class when the Holy Spirit shined a light in my heart and said, "You're selfish!" I argued with him LOL. He said it again. I walked out of class crying so hard and went into the bathroom repenting.

I repented.

When God exposes your heart to you, it's just better to repent and admit it. He does that so that we can see it and deal with it.

He cleans our heart out for many reasons. One is so that we can forgive others. Another is so that we are not deceived. When we allow bitterness to set in and unforgiveness, it will cause us to operate in jealousy, anger, wrath, malice, and many other sins. It develops a root and many other expressions come out of it.

I encourage you Bride to deal with these roots and allow God to heal you and take you to the next level. This next level of warfare requires that we shut all the doors and gates to the enemy. The time has come to drop all these things that so easily beset us from fulfilling our destiny. How many of us desire to stand before our holy judge and hear Him say, "Well done thy good and faithful servant!" Notice the key word "servant".

Beware of that Old Serpent – King of Pride

Another way pride affects us is unforgiveness. We can't be a servant if we're filled with pride. Therefore, Satan attacks us where it hurts so that we will not bend our knee to God and to others.

Pride causes us to be puffed up and to where we have guards up. It also puts us up on platforms to where we are higher than others. It also surrounds us with people who keep us puffed up on that platform. This is a dangerous situation.

Think of the two main players on the scene right now and their pride level – Kanye & President Trump. Kanye says they're both filled with dragon energy. Kanye's pride declares he's the best ever created (or so he says at Joel Osteen's church). Kanye is one of the main faces now of the one world religion. He is being used to pull everyone together with the support of the evangelicals. We all know Trump's pride level. Trump is being representative of the Beast. He is the arm of the political/governmental aspect of the end times. We will talk about this connection later. Both of these men are highly promoted by the NAR (New Apostolic Reformation) evangelicals. **Note – both men visited the Pope at the Vatican in 2016 before both were activated into the agenda. Guess who else was at the Vatican the past few years? THE EVANGELICALS! The very ones who are with the President and supporting Kanye! They're all in this together! Be knowledgeable of the time you are in Bride.

As we step into this royal moment of time, it's not about fame and fortune, it is about going lower. We must stay on our face before God so that He can keep us grounded and humble. The devil is the one who wants to puff us up and cause us to think that we are higher than we are. He tries to convince us that we do not need faith or God. I will talk about this more later.

What About the Time I've Lost?

I hear some of you asking this. There's not anything we can do about the past. It is history. God knows this. However, He can redeem the time.

Once you lay it all down and give him THE TIME YOU HAVE LEFT, He can make the most out of that.

He is the one who holds our tomorrows and knows how much time we have left. However, whether we have five minutes or five years left, it's His!

TIME PROPHETICALLY

We are in the last days Bride. I don't care what any other person or ministry is teaching people. The Bible is the truth. It's not racist, biased, or misrepresented by God. The Bible spells out a time scenario that is totally opposite of what these groups are teaching.

Get ready Bride because the time has come for us to step out and defend the word of God and the TRUTH in this hour! A false worldwide movement is about to happen, and we must know what the word says and use it as your sword! Souls are hanging in the balance and time is on our side! You know why? It's because God is with us! We can do more with Him at the wheel than 10 more years of our own powers!

Lock and Load Bride! This is YOUR ROYAL MOMENT OF TIME!

It was an honor to serve the Bride in Washington DC

2
Terms & Definitions

FYI for last days apostasy

Matthew 24:24 – For there shall arise false Christs, and false prophets, and shall shew great signs and wonders; insomuch that, if it were possible, they shall deceive even the elect.

As I try to explain the condition of the church and all the things that the Lord has revealed to me, I must begin by defining terms so that you understand as to what I'm referring to. In the Christian world, we have a lot of "Christianese", and I'll try very hard to avoid those terms and be as simple as I can. My heart's desire is that you will understand this great apostasy and be able to make the right decision. These definitions are what I have gathered through my tons of research and just my way of describing it.

• **Smart Devices – (Alexa, Google Home, etc**.) – These are devices that the enemy (the worldly Beast) is putting in your home to secretly listen to your conversations. They are recording everything. Data is the #1 commodity on the planet. They want to know all about you and use it against you later.

• **Apostasy** – the final deceitful plan of the enemy/Devil to deceive and lie to God's people and cause them to have blinders on their eyes and not see the truth. It is the devil's plan to fool them and take them down a wrong path and send massive amounts of people to Hell. It means an abandonment of their faith. Leaving the truth.

• **Black Liberation Theology** – I could write a whole book on this theology. Basically, it is the liberal side for the black church. It's very un-Christian. They try to say that Christianity is favorable towards white people and is the white people's religion (or that they hijacked it). They paint Jesus as black. They try to fight for their injustices but really, it's a form of a hatred group. This causes people to be divided due to prejudices being reversed. Black people now racist to white people. It's a twisting. In other words, it doesn't help, it makes it worse. This is Barack Hussein Obama's pastor's teachings. It explains a lot of his presidency.

• **Catholic** –There are two kinds of Catholics. The Roman Catholics (the Pope) and the Orthodox. See, the Christians go by the Holy Bible and preferably the King James version. This Bible is a different book than the Catholics use. They use their Bible which includes additional books called the Apocrypha. When King James formed a team of 50 scholars to publish an English Bible, they left out those books because they said it was not "inspired by God". They also had other criteria such as if it matched the other books, etc. The Catholics tried to assassinate King James many times to no avail. It's a very interesting story and I pray you study it out. The Catholic Church worships idols and practices sacrilege things. It also controls most all things on the Earth. They are powerful with a billion followers. You will learn more in this book how they (the Vatican) is behind the one world order and religion.

16

- **Charismatic** – It is like Pentecostalism in that they believe in speaking in tongues and the gifts of the Holy Spirit. This movement highlights the gifts of the Holy Spirit. They are known as charismatic and emotional to others because of the manifestations. This group is also known as the glory stream. They are accused of seeking after signs, miracles and wonders versus solid biblical doctrine. For instance, their churches did away with Sunday School.

- **Coexist** – All religions to come together as one in a false love. They want to become one in the Earth. Co-exist means to have tolerance, understanding, and inclusion of all people but Christians (the fundamental ones – the ones who believe the Bible for what it says). They believe in conducting dialogue between different religions and faith based upon Humanism (putting the humans above God). Social justice is their cry.

- **Common Good & Dialogue** – This is a Roman Catholic term that you need to know because this is what they say when they are trying to do the false unity in the Earth. They are trying to pull different religions together by agreeing to a "common good" of social justice and earthly change. The dialogue part means that they want this interreligious group to come together and talk about their differences with respect and in the understanding of coming together in this unity. This will lead to the one-world religion. They hate individualism. They do not want everyone to consider the bigger picture over individual people. This will be the excuse on why they can kill Christians in future because it will help "The Common Good" or "The Community." You need to watch that movie *The Circle* with Tom Hanks.

- **Contemplative Prayer** – This is a Catholic/mystical form of prayer in which a person quiets their mind, contemplates on God through visions in their head. They say chants and repeats a word or phrase repeatedly while they have a picture in their head of it. It may be Heaven and the throne room, or it may be visualizing what Jesus looks like. This form of prayer opens you up to demonic spirits. You are emptying your mind and it is not scriptural. They try to say that you should "be still and know that I am God". However, this scripture is about our actions when we are in of God's will. Be still and trust that God is going to move on your behalf. (Thus, why we cannot do the Courts of Heaven). Contemplative Prayer also opens you up to the Kundalini spirit (false Jesus, false holy spirit). It does take you into an intoxicating bliss state, but it is satanic to the core and not holy. It is an eastern religion practice. The root of it is Catholic, Hinduism and New Age. This causes the person to look like "a hippy". It is like they are high all the time. It is a false joy.

• **Courts of Heaven** – This is where Christians astral-project out of their body and travel through the heavens to the 3rd Heaven into the courts and they fight for their own lives in the courtroom. They battle Satan and his demons. God renders a judgment on their behalf then they travel back to Earth into their bodies and now they are victorious. Like gods they have more control of their own destiny. No more do they trust in Jesus to fight their battles for them. No longer do they have to wait upon the Lord, they have more power to take things into their own hands. In addition, soul-travel is witchcraft and occult. It is Satanic to the core! Do not do this! They may say it's only visualization, but the point is that it's all mystical. Sadly this practice is growing tremendously in the Charismatic church. (glory stream). It is another form of Dominionism.

• **Deliverance** – This means the casting out demons out of a human. Delivering them from evil spirits.

18

•   **Discernment** - This is the Holy Spirit helping a person to know what is right and wrong in God's eyes based upon the word of God and the infilling of the Holy Ghost. The Holy Spirit is our teacher and guide. He's the only guide we need. This is a knowing of what is right and wrong supernaturally. However, spirit guides are from the occult (New Age mostly).

•   **Dominionism** – This is a theology that we have dominion in the Earth through spiritual authority. We are of another kingdom. We are children of God. This goes along with the word of faith religion in which we can speak with our mouth and cause things to happen because we are the sons and daughters of God. Because we are married to Christ, we have authority as His Bride. We have all rights to the Kingdom. This I believe myself. However, where it goes off into heresy is when they try to use this authority against God's will. For instance, we know that God says in the last days we will experience wars and rumors of wars. Do we use our dominion authority to speak to that war and tell it to stop? Do we go against the will of God? It's a fine line. What God means by using His authority is where He says, "In my name you will cast out devils, speak to the mountain and tell it to go (meaning obstacles in your life against God's will), stomp on scorpions, etc." This means that we are not bound by natural law when it comes to fulfilling our destiny. The key is knowing if it is God's will. A great example of taking authority when it's in God's will is like one-time God told me to go out of state and serve this ministry. I was driving an old car, and everyone was saying that car will not make it and they were mocking me and God. I said, "If God told me to go it will make it". I was on the phone with a minister who heard the car banging and clanging about to fall apart and she said, "You're not going to make it." When I got off the phone with her this righteous indignation come over me and I slammed my fist on that dash and I screamed, "In the name of Jesus, you will run and take me to North Carolina! I command you to work and obey the will of the Lord! God told me to go and YOU WILL TAKE ME THERE in the name of Jesus!" After I finished a miracle happened. The car straightened up, the check engine light went off, and it drove me like a brand-new car all the way from Nashville to North Carolina! If I was on that mission, that car ran like a brand-new car! However, when I arrived back in Nashville and my mission was over, the car went back to the way it was! This is the correct way to use Dominionism. The wrong way is this, "I command a car to be sitting in my driveway tomorrow in Jesus name! I will not stand for less!" NAR has twisted this revelation. Their version of Dominionism says that we will take over the whole world and bring a Utopia in the world and no end of times is coming. It partners with this idea that a great revival is coming and going to be BLISS all over the world. In other words, we do have dominion if we use it right. Not against God's will. This also partners with the seven-mountain mandate of taking over the seven mountains of culture in the world to have control. Instead of going after souls, they are going after the earthly benefits. They believe they must take over the seven spheres of society across the whole world and create a perfect world before Jesus returns. The sad truth is that the world they're creating is for the Antichrist. God didn't tell us to save systems. He said to save souls. If we spent as much energy on souls as we do politics and cities, etc., we would have the whole world saved by now. Think about it.

• **Drones** – These are aircraft that they will use to spy on you in the future. These vary in size. They can be as small as a mosquito and have a camera attached. The government may use them to spy on you. I write about this in my *Mark of the Beast* book and more in *The Last American Bride* book. Right now they allow people to purchase them so you will not be able to distinguish.

• **Ecumenical** – This means the Roman Catholic Church is blending with all religions to form the One World Religion by coming together to form a "dialogue" across denominational and religious boundaries. They are blurring the lines of truth to do "Social Justice" and to achieve their mandate of a mass missions for the Pope and the One World Religion. I believe the Seven (7) Mountain mandate plays in this. It is False Unity because it cannot be sanctioned by the God of Abraham Isaac & Jacob. God hates mixing; thus, they are mixing. They call it Interfaith movement. Coexisting with other faiths, etc. The dark truth is that the Catholic Church wants all the world under the mother church. All roads lead back to Rome. It's unholy and will end up being the avenue in which Christians are martyred in the future. Really, they have infiltrated the church and become all things to all people. There is a right-side branch of the Ecumenical Movement (NAR) and left side (Emergent). They are all speaking the same language and it all comes back to Rome. The evangelicals in the White House and mainly from the glory stream has partnered with this. They are merging everyone together AS ONE. Also, the Noahide Laws play into this as well. They are a part of the AS ONE (Orthodox Jews). Do you believe it is ironic that Kanye is using Catholic symbols in his clothing sales and images on the platform? What about his promotions of the Catholic Church and the United Nations? Yes he has talked about both of them in interviews.

• **Elitism (tribes, etc.)** – This is one of the idols we repented about. This is where people think they are better than others. They form these cliques and think they are superheroes and better than other people. It's kind of like a secret society like Masons or Illuminati. God does not want us thinking more highly of ourselves or causing others to feel slighted. He says in His word that we are not to prefer other people over other people. (2 Chronicles 12). We are not to show favoritism and separate like that. Think about what He said about the poor and how they are to be treated in the church. Same concept. Many people judge based upon finances or outward appearance and God does not endorse that. Many of these write books about different spirits to be paranoid about. They teach you to "beware" "toxic" "Jezebel", etc. It's all to exclude you in relationships and bring trust to your new leaders. This is why they partnered with Kanye West so quick. Their pride level and being like superhero's partners with the Kanye spirit. No humbleness. Also isn't it funny how NAR pushes the TITLES of apostle, prophet, teacher, etc.? Notice the correlation of that and the Catholic Church that they have now partnered with. It's all a hierarchy.

• **Emergent Church** – The Emergent Church is a satanic move to spew vomit into people through watering down the gospel. They're trying to make it easier for people to accept Jesus. This group went to the extreme when it comes to bringing the world in the church. This represents progressive Christianity. The liberal side. One of their tactics is through mixing various religions into one. This is Ecumenical to the core. They will mix New Age ceremonies into their services such as Yoga and the Labyrinth. They will also do Catholicism things such as candles, Eucharist, idols, and other things. They are trying to attract the Millennials by watering down the gospel to the hilt. They have dialogue instead of preaching. You walk in their church and there is couches everywhere, dress down, and the leader sits in the middle and asks questions instead of teaching them the Bible. They do speak in tongues and act like they have the miracles signs and wonders, but it's all fake because God can never be with idolatry and mixing with other religions. I will explain more in a later section. They are very worldly and do not want to offend anyone. They are very inclusive. Really, they are repackaged Catholicism. Most all of them participate in the Eucharist communion ceremony and practice other mystical Catholic traditions. Basically they have blended all "good" things from all the religions together under one umbrella. Also consider at one of Kanye's Sunday Services he rebuked the church for discernment in ministries such as TD Jakes, Mormons, etc. In other words he is talking about dropping all doctrine. He was preaching that we have made Christianity too hard and he has it right. Watch the video here - https://www.youtube.com/watch?v=zyU3NM5MPqc.

• **Great Revival Coming – Awakening** – At first I thought it was only the Christian version of Kingdom of God movement is using to bring a false peace to the church. They are striving to say that we have this huge revival coming and great days are ahead. They are saying it like Utopia is ahead. However, after being in Washington I realize their version of Kingdom of God is not what we think it is. Did you know that the LGBTQ is calling this the Great Awakening? Why? Because the President has merged them with the Evangelicals, conservatives, etc. New Age is proclaiming a great awakening time called Golden Age when the messiah comes (we know as Antichrist). So, it's a merger of FALSE LOVE. Salvation is nowhere in the picture. This is a false theology because the Bible states we are headed into a great falling away. We will have a revival, but it will be nothing like they are saying. It will be in great suffering and the only revival it will be is of God's mercy in true desperation. Yes, God will use us mightily, but it will not be in the arrogant way the *NAR – Kingdom Now* people suggest. I believe there is a false revival coming and it will spread this virus like crazy. It will be a revival of false love and unity. We will probably have to go underground at that time. Or, another scenario would be that two revivals are taking place at the same time. A false one (strange manifestations, false love, universalism, bliss, signs miracles & wonders, and Christ-consciousness – New Age Jesus). In the meantime, the real one (truth, persecution, true signs miracles and wonders, and death). The true God will receive the glory and not man or a group, tribe, or network and surely not the Catholic Church. It appears that the false one is being led now by Kanye West with the evangelicals in partnership with the world system. They are all celebrating him. This is a true sign of a false evangelical. He partners with UN, pluralism, globalism, Pope, feelings-only, no repentance, pride and power. Sounds a lot like President Trump huh? Look at that description again. The same evangelicals that surround Trump surround Kanye. Both men are prideful, boast they are the best and according to Kanye, they're both Dragons.

• **Heavenly Realm** – There are many levels of heaven. 1st heaven is here on Earth. 2nd heaven is right above our heads and past the stars which is where the principalities and powers are. This is where the spiritual warfare is taking place (angels and demons). Then the 3rd heaven is where God and his elders are. This level is where people go when they die (the ones that made it to heaven). So, when people say heavenly realm, they mean the 3rd one.

• **Hinduism** – This religion is based in India and includes over 33 million gods. This is the 3rd largest religion in the world. To them it is more of a lifestyle, but they include many different types of religion such as polytheistic, pantheistic, monotheistic, monistic, agnostic, atheistic or humanist. They are well-known for being the roots of Yoga.

• **Humanism** – this is a movement that puts human reasoning and life above God. It places more emphasis on the human element rather than God and the supernatural. (faith). It waves the banner of social justice to help mankind but does not want spiritual help. Man over God.

• **Idols** – these are things that we trust in when we are hurting instead of God. The official definition is a person or thing that is greatly revered, loved or adored. I submit that it can also be ideologies or images as well.

• **Illuminati** – The secret society controlling the world. They are behind the major forces such as the media, entertainment, education, etc. They push their agenda to one day enforce the One World Order. They are real.

• **Inclusive** – means that they "include" everyone to include any faith such as Muslims, Jews, Witches (Wicca), LGBTQ community (homosexuals), Catholics, any way you want to describe your gender, etc. They are inclusive with no boundaries. This word is also used in the fake "love" revival. Love is not exclusive with sin in God's eyes. Love is truth. Love is obedience. They also paint "love" as the "universe or community".

• **Interfaith** – This means the blending of all the faiths into one, which is basically New Age religion. It's a feel-good religion where there is no judging and no lines to cross. Utopia of fleshly desires with no limits.

• **Internet of Things** – This is a codeword action they are using to make all of this happen. Their goal is to make everything on the planet connected through the internet. They want machines, appliances, cars, electronics, phones, and even you all talking to each other. This is so that you will ALL be a part of the new "community".

• **Jesuits** – (Society of Jesus) – Apparently, they are the army of the Roman Catholic Church. They are like a secret service for the Vatican. They are OVER the Illuminati, International Bankers, Masons, etc. They have been known (or at least highly suspected) to kill kings and presidents. They enforce the Roman Catholic Church's evil agendas.

• **Judgment** – Judgment is God removing his hand to allow his people to see what the world would be like without his protection. He removes his hand of protection and allows the enemy to have more access to his people. In other words, as a father, He is allowing mankind to see the repercussions of their own sins and choices. God has revealed to mankind time and time again in the Old Testament how his heart is about sin. By God's hand being upon us, we are blessed beyond measure. It's only his grace that we have been protected all this time. When he removes His hand, then the very Earth will have justice on the sin and blood that has been shed on it. Through judgment, natural disasters happen, famine, pestilence, and violence. There is nothing holy holding it back anymore. See, Christians do not realize the bubble they are in when they are in obedience. However, judgment comes to those who are in disobedience and rebellion. The Bible calls them stiff-necked. I hosted a program explaining how God produced judgments in the Old Testament. His pattern is the same. More later...

• **King James Bible** – As noted above, King James published this book for the English people in 1611. After surviving assignation attempts from the Catholics, he finally provided the English-speaking people the ability to see what God had to say about things versus what the Catholic Church tried to force on people. King James formed groups out of the top 50 Hebrew and Greek scholars of the day to examine the scrolls and decipher it to our language. They then rotated certain books between the teams to insure accuracy. This is the book that is basically the root of all other bibles. I highly endorse this version because as you will learn in this book, the enemy has produced many other versions and its deceiving mankind. However, I do recommend (since I am a publisher and understand how they do this), that you pay very close attention to who the publisher is because they may have a Satanic agenda. I do not recommend Zondervan or Charisma Publishers. Versions I do not recommend for sure are MEV, Passion, NAS, RSV, The Spirit-Filled Bible, and Reformation Bible. See, the Ecumenical Movement is pushing their agenda through published works such as books and Bibles.

•   **Kingdom of God** –There is a Kingdom of God, it is within us. It does encompass the whole Bride of Christ – not the fake one – universal. You will know the difference by if they're mixing with the ecumenical movement and Co-exist movement or not.

•   **Kundalini** – It is a serpent spirit that lays dormant at the base of the spine and wraps around the spine and goes all the way up to the third eye which is located between the two front eyes on the head. In New Age and Hinduism, this is highly prevalent. They work to activate the Chakras. Chakras are seven energy points in your body and when awakened, (usually through Yoga and meditation), then it brings a feeling of Utopia and euphoria. This serpent spirit is passed through many ways, but mainly through laying on of hands on the head. The manifestations resemble the Holy Spirit. There are two main differences. The manifestation from this false one results in violent ticks or shakes. It's one thing to shake in the presence of the Lord than to be a violent shake that looks demonic. I will explain more later. The spirit looks like a hippy. They look like they're drunk or high all the time. It's referred to as the Serpent Spirit. It's unholy. It is not the Holy Ghost. It is a seductive spirit. When a snake bites, it causes like an intoxicating feeling before it kills. I believe this is Leviathan spirit.

• **Labyrinth** – A labyrinth is like a big puzzle they draw on the floor and they try to say that it increases your prayer life the closer you move in to the center, but it is Witchcraft and Occult. Not good. It looks like a big circle with lines all in it to reveal the inner circle. They also use this as a form of "centering prayer", which is mystical as well.

• **Leviathan** – This is one of the chief demons. This is a principality. It is one of the seven principalities in the 2nd heaven. It is the serpent demon and it is the chief demon of pride. This is behind tattoos and piercings. This spirit twists truth and things that people say and the words of God.

• **LGBTQ** – This means lesbian, gays, bi-sexual, transgender and those that question who they are. This acronym is not people. It is a demonic spirit agenda. It seeks to pervert mankind so they will not know their identity in Christ. Did you know their capitol is in Israel? Shocker huh? Also…did you know that Israel and America is on the board at the United Nations to push the LGBTQ agenda? Shocker! We cannot partner with this spirit.

• **Manifest Sons of God** – This is a term mis-used by the NAR in which they mean that humans that are saved, filled with the Holy Ghost, will mature to a level where they will manifest as sons and daughters of God. This means walking in the authority of heaven and doing miraculous works. I do agree that we will all mature into his sons and daughters of God and be used mightily by Him, but their term means a little different. This apologetics website defines it as, "The teaching that in the last days, a "new breed" of Christians will arise - the "Manifest Sons of God" - who will have super-natural spiritual power and be instrumental in subduing the Earth. This movement is also referred to as "Joel's Army." 'Subduing the Earth' means that a militant church (Joel's Army) will arise, take over and rule the world politically and spiritually. It is claimed that the 'Manifest Sons of God' will be perfected into their "glorified bodies" prior to Christ's return. That perfection will allow them to subdue the Earth for Jesus. Proponents of this doctrine also claim Christians, having a "divine nature," become "gods." They say Christ came into us as a "seed" and grows into a "prophet." Thus, Christ does not physically return, but returns within us. The rapture, according to this doctrine, will be of the wicked - not of believers. (Apologetics Index, 2018)

• **Mark of the Beast** – This is the mark that the Beast is going to implement during the Tribulation period. This will be to label each person for the beast. In my theory, this mark will be the human implantation chip (RFID). Do not take the mark! You will be automatically doomed for Hell and have no chance for salvation once you take it. It's in Book of Revelation. 666. The Internet of Things agenda (UN Agenda 2030) is being implemented now and will require all humans to have the CHIP implanted on the inside of them so that they will be able to buy and sell in this new global economy and community. THE BEAST.

• **Masons (Freemasonry)** – This is a fraternal organization that traces their roots to the Roman Catholic Church. They are a secret society in which they climb levels in obedience to the ceremonies and initiations. By the time they get to the 32nd & 33rd degree, it is revealed that Lucifer is the "Enlightened One". It is a Satanic and unholy organization. When you're in it, they say the only way out is death. I have discovered that most of those deaths are through auto accidents. In the worldly sense though, when you join this group, it opens doors amazingly. You gain higher power in the world. You are greatly respected in worldly realms. You are bypassed on crimes, etc. (This is all not exact fact…this is just my studies remember).

• **Missiology**- This is the doctrine of missions or the belief of how a certain people should do mission work. This is a plan to take over the world through the Ecumenical Movement and the Pope.

• **Mysticism** – This is a term Christians should run from. This mainly comes from the Roman Catholic, Orthodox Catholic, Hindu, or New Age religion. This is a mystical/magical connotation. It's another word for supernatural but in the wrong way. The Bible labels it as Jewish fables as well. Titus 1:4

• **New Age** – It is a religion counterfeit to the word of God. This was founded by a lady who left Christianity and exclaimed that now you need to find the god within yourself through their consciousness. They believe that each person is a god within and in the "universe". It wants to become one with the universe. It includes Yoga, essential oils, meditation, etc. It has moral relativism, which means there is no right and wrong and it is all bliss in this world. It is very inclusive of all religions and has a specific hate towards Christianity because we have absolutes (word of God). This has infiltrated the church and society. The Ecumenical Movement (EM), Emergent Church (EC) and New Apostolic Reformation (NAR) is full of it! Many in the church world have included this in their church.

• **New Apostolic Reformation (NAR)** – This group believes that the current church system is in grave error to the word of God. They will often preach that the word "pastor" is only used in the bible a few times. They feel like the church should go back to the five-fold ministry standard of the apostle, prophet, pastor, evangelist, and teacher. I do agree with them in that the church has very serious issues that God is not happy about right now. The preacher-pyramid that has been in existence for a while has stifled many Christians from achieving their God-given destiny is a serious issue. However, their answer for it is not the right one. So, this group believes that a new order is coming to the Earth to rid this dry, dead old system to a new apostolic order. They believe that they are now raising up apostolic hubs and centers ran by apostles. These apostles are most of the time self-appointed and they will commission others to go out and do their own mission. They equip and send out. They may be small, but they are growing. It's really a form of rebellion because they are doing the same thing they are accusing the church about. They are saying that the traditional church is not in right order when, they are doing the same thing! They are creating their own order. This group is also bringing persecution against the term "Christianity" and painting a bad light on it. This is because they want to control the narrative. (Kingdom). Most of this group is preterist doctrine – meaning they believe no Tribulation is coming and Jesus is coming back to reign in the temple. They believe they are preparing the world for Jesus to return so Christians must takeover everything. (7 mountain mandate). False teaching. They do not teach on proper eschatology, sin, consequences to sin and they partner with other religions, LGBTQ, inclusive and many teach the Tree of Knowledge of Good and Evil does not even exist anymore. Jesus paid it all on the cross so you do not have to overcome sin.

• **Pentecostal(ism)** – the movement of being filled with the Holy Ghost and speaking in tongues. Most non- denominational churches are Pentecostal. They speak in tongues and believe in the gifts of the spirit.

• **Pope** – The head of the Roman Catholic Church. It's their head Bishop. The Catholic Church sees him as the successor to the Apostle Peter. He is the authority head of the entire church. The current Pope is Pope Frances and he is the 45th Pope. Many prophecies that he is the last one! Notice lately all the movies and documentaries about him? I believe it's preparing the way for global worship!

• **Preacher Pyramid** – this is where a pastor will run a church by himself with no board and try to control everything like a tyrant. This person (whether man or woman) will want everyone under them to serve their vision only. They quit discipling and causing people to discover their own mission that God may have for them. These ministers build their own kingdom (use the money for the kingdom to buy big houses and live large while people are suffering in community. They will use the money for greed). The people that attend their church may sit in that same church 30-50 years and not do anything. This is grave error because we are commissioned to raise up disciples. They are modeling this after the catholic church where they have a priest, and everyone just sits there. God has called each person for a mission and it may be to serve that pastor's vision, but without them having the opportunity to learn for themselves, how will they know? This means that he is not a servant to the body, they are servants to him (or her). They are not raising up to send out. It's a power structure. However, you will notice that the NAR is complaining about this but they're doing the same thing. Ironic. God is about to shake "the system". He may bring us all back to house churches like in the Book of Acts. I do believe we will have to go underground because the churches will be so infiltrated with the filth.

• **Proselytize** – This is an attempt to try to convert someone form one religion to another. Means to evangelize and convert. Save. In California they just passed a law banning Christians from doing this to the LGBTQ community and from trying to do any conversion therapy, healing or delivering them. Also, the Pope really pushes for the people in the ecumenical movement are not allowed to proselytize. Zionists do not want you to proselytize Jews either.

• **Prosperity Gospel** – this has surely received a bad light because of the overuse of money and greed many TV preachers have displayed that preach this doctrine. Basically, they teach that it is God's will for you to be prosperous and healthy. This part is true. God wants you prosper and be in health. That is the word. The problem becomes when they abuse the Body of Christ with it and make a mockery out of Jesus name. For instance, when someone is suffering due to a lack in the church, they are often viewed as non-faithful, faithless, lacking, loser, and as I was told one time – I am immature. If I was more mature, I would have wealth. What people don't consider is that obedience is the key to various kinds of wealth. Through obedience God may have you suffer as you are in your testing. In that case, this movement will view you as a faithless person or you're not doing something right. What they forget is that Jesus told the rich man, "Give away everything you have and follow me." (Matt. 19:21). Money and material things should not be our goal. Wealth is so much more than money or material things. In the prosperity gospel however, this is not preached. There are many other reasons this is viewed in such a bad light and one of them is how the big-named preachers will charge for prophetic words and try to entice the church to give large sums of money for a reward. This is heretical and a stench in God's nostrils. This also has a negative light in how they do not help the poor and cause them to feel disenfranchised in the Body of Christ due to this doctrine. I must say however that God does want us to prosper but we are not to be greedy or hoard our things and money. God wants to use us as a conduit to help the kingdom. We do not own anything. Our house, car, church, ministry, clothes, furniture, land, or anything else we own is not ours. It's all God's and he may ask for it back. He may want you to bless someone else with it. The prosperity gospel does not teach this. Just remember though that God does want us in health and to prosper. (3 John 1:2). We must ensure the prosperity does not take our heart.

• **RFID – Radio Frequency Identification Device** – This is the mark of the beast. It is a chip that they will insert under your skin and it implants into your tissue and becomes part of your insides. It is basically a device that links us to the beast of this world (internet and computers). Their goal is to make us man-to-machine. They want everything on the Earth to be connected to the Beast. You can read my book, *Mark of the Beast*, which sells at www.gotreehouse.org.

• **Seven Mountain Mandate** – This is a theology produced by some ministers who coined this term by exploring the idea that we can change our culture by focusing on the seven cultural areas such as government, arts & entertainment, media, education, family, business, & religion. The NAR is behind this belief. They want to take control of these mountains to control society and create a kingdom on Earth. The harm in this is that they do not believe in the correct eschatology. They believe that in order for Jesus to come back, that we must take over the entire seven mountains and create a Christian Earth before Jesus can return. This is false because the Earth is in process of preparing for the Antichrist.

•   **Slain in the Spirit** – I have heard some disagree and say this is not biblical, but God slain Saul on the road to Damascus. It means where a person falls under the power of God, whether they are being prayed for or not. Sometimes people have been slain with no one around. It falls under the false if it has strange manifestations with it like violent jerks, barking, howling, etc. (demonic manifestations).

•   **Social Media** –In the beginning of the internet it was only one way of communication. People put things on their websites and you read it and maybe contacted them by phone or email. Then when it evolved, it became where it can be real-time interaction on both sides. Now we have social media which means that media is now social. (Facebook, Snapchat, Twitter, YouTube, Myspace, etc.)

•   **Tattoos & Piercings** – The reason these are mentioned is because I did a *Clarion Call* show about the epidemic of tattoos and the root of them. I noticed it in massive numbers in the church as I traveled the nation. The Body of Christ has been infiltrated with people getting tattoos and piercings. It is growing at an alarming rate. You will see ministers on Facebook and other LIVE programs showing off their tattoos and they will even look at them while they're talking. You can tell its self-adoration. How many of them do you see showing off their tattoos on their profile pictures? It's because when I interviewed Dr. Phillip Morris of Restoration Church in Highlands Texas, he explained that when someone gets a tattoo, they are opening themselves up to demons. He further explained that Leviathan, the chief demon of pride, is what enters the person when they get a tattoo. Therefore, they will get addicted and get more and more. Also, why they must "show it off" to the world. It is a pride issue. He further explained how piercings open the door as well. You will see as I talk about the NAR movement that this is where you will see many with tattoos because one of the fruits of this movement is pride and arrogance.

o **The Kingdom of God** – this Kingdom is in opposite of the other one. It is by the rule of God. In this Kingdom we abide by God's laws and it always supersedes the Earthly realm. This Kingdom comes with promises that we have access to and we can use as the Bride of Christ (healing, provision, angelic help, etc.). So, when we know who we are In Christ, then we can have all the access to this Kingdom's provisions here on Earth. The problem becomes when we use this term against the Christians and I will talk about this later. They are wanting to do away with the term "Christianity" and replace it with "Kingdom of God" because the KOG term they can be inclusive with other heretical doctrines. (Or so they think, and it is not biblical). This term is part of the apostasy.

o **The Kingdom of this World** – this is the unseen realm that controls the actual worldly system through the Spirit of Antichrist. This operates with an evil agenda and means to lure the humans to Satan's agenda and eventually send them to Hell. In this kingdom, they will grant their participants great things, but one day they will have to pay the piper. It has an identity for each person and this one is more "accepted" in the Earth. They use many ways to influence man – media, advertising, movies, educational system, and music. This road always leads to death. Through this world it controls what you see. This is where Satan fools people. He controls their sight so that they trust it more than what they do not see, which is the next kingdom and requires faith.

- **Witchcraft & Occult** – This is Satanic in nature. We are not to touch this or mix with it. This includes watching it, etc. It is a false religion that relies on divination and other abominable acts that God hates. This includes fortune telling, palm reading, Ouija Board, tarot cards etc. The Witchcraft specifically can include Harry Potter and other forms of magic. It is a form of control in which the person that operates it feels empowered because demons work on their behalf; thus, they cast spells and astral-project their soul out of their body.

- **Word of Faith Movement** – I was in this for over 30 years. Word of Faith means that we can use our mouth to speak things into existence. It means to name it and claim it. It has received a bad name because they mixed it with Prosperity Gospel. I will explain that next. However, word of faith is very much true. Our mouth can bring sickness, faith, depression, cursing, blessings, etc. I am going to write a book one day about how it affected my mother. I know this first hand. The Bible says that out of the mouth the heart speaks. We must tame it and speak words of LIFE and healing. Well, I can see as well how many can think negative of this as well because many speak ONLY positive and are not real about the situations. For instance, I was going to a WOF church and in a terrible abusive marriage. I couldn't talk about it with anyone because I was "hushed" and assured not to speak negative. However, I was hurting. Help me Lord. So, on that side I can see how it can hurt people if they cannot confess their sins one to another and express how they feel. It tends to bring a fake Christianity because they're always speaking what's not true in the now. However, to the person who really believes this doctrine, they are speaking what they want to happen. So, let it be according to their faith and it is scriptural.

- **Yoga**– Both of them are in the New Age religion. The Yoga stems from Hinduism. Yoga is where you move your body to different positions to summon gods. Each position is strategic. It is Satanic to the core. New Age is a perverted and twisted type of spirituality. It is a blend of all religions. Many in the NAR act like people high on dope at New Age festivals. It's that "hippie" spirit I will describe later. New Age is partnered with the spirit of antichrist, masons, united nations, etc.

• **Noahide Laws** – These are seven (7) made-up laws by the Orthodox Jews. They are working the United Nations and world leaders to implement these laws worldwide. When they implement these laws Christians will be martyred. If you commit blasphemy (which we will when we do not renounce Jesus Christ), then we will be beheaded. The sad thing is that President Trump, the evangelicals in the White House, Benjamin Netanyahu and the Pope all go along with this plan. They are all in this together. I will present my case and findings in this book to explain this to you. Study www.noahide.org. They have an institute that pushes this agenda across the world. Another sad fact is that the leaders of the NAR group are doing videos to tell their followers that there is nothing to fear with the Noahide Laws. This is not a conspiracy theory. Check out UN.org.

• **Eschatology** – what people believe concerning the end of times. This is a belief system about the last day events. This is very important to ask your pastor what do they believe because everything they preach is based on this belief. If a church does not believe the Tribulation seven-year period is coming, they will preach differently. For instance, I know the Antichrist is coming so my preaching will be warning the church and preparing them for rough days ahead. Please ask your leaders.

o **How will you know true from false?**

☐ Doctrine – do they even have doctrine and does it match Bible?

☐ Are they in the EM? Who are their associations?

☐ What is their fruit?

☐ Are they mixing with New Age or Occult? Worldly things?

☐ Are they inclusive?

Dr. June Dawn Knight

3

Condition of the Church

Situation Room – Spiritual Warfare

This book is dedicated to the church here in the United States of America. The reason it is not focused globally is because of the nature of our culture and the spiritually important role our nation plays in the last days. We have a covenant with God and He has a plan for us. He wants to use our people to speak truth to other nations who do not know Jesus – including the Jews. Our people and our land will be held accountable to God for the sins placed upon this nation. As a church, we must examine honestly the condition of the church and our nation.

Current Condition of the Church

When I was on the MAGA (Making America Godly Again) Tour in 2017, God revealed this sickness in the church. It hurt my heart to see it. Now I'm going to tell you what that sickness is and how it is affecting the church and America as a whole. As I stated earlier, this is probably true of the entire planet, but the target audience for this book is our own country, the United States of America.

The Lord told me when He gave me the assignment in February of 2017 that I am to focus on the nation spiritually.

In addition to the *MAGA Revival tour*, this observation of our country is based upon what God has revealed to me through my many years on the road throughout the country, the word of God, and in prayer.

We are Sick

How do we define the soul of our country? Well, let's examine the current day news. In addition to all the chaos happening in our country, what about what God revealed through prayer praying for our country? WATB (We are the Bride) Ministries did a *50 Dayz a Blaze* Prayer Initiative in 2017 where we prayed for each state while I was on the road. We prayed every day for 50 days. During this time, it was revealed the state's individual challenges and stronghold and we prayed about it.

Opioid Crisis

One of those symptoms is the Opioid crisis in our country. This is a drug epidemic that is taking place and killing thousands upon thousands of people through drug addiction! When we were deep in warfare over our states, we became keenly aware of this tragedy happening in our country. I can understand why Melania Trump is so adamant on coming up with a solution. However, I must concur that this is a terrible reflection on the church. Do you see how we are to blame to God for this?

All these people are bound up in demons and we are not out there casting demons out. We are not even preaching in the church not to do this or what sin will do to take them that far.

People need relief and as the Body of Christ, we have a duty to God to help people find relief and healing. Real Christianity is outward-focused (others).

The reason that most churches are not delivering people is because they have built their own kingdoms. They're so busy trying to build their own kingdom that they are not doing what God called them to do. According to Prophet Sadhu Selvaraj's preaching in Australia last year in September, "If you're a minister of God, quit building your own kingdom. Quit having a very self-centered viewpoint. Don't have this idea of 'my church, my service', 'my tithes', 'my offerings'. That my my my must die." (Selvaraj, 2018) Inside the churches has become a bless-me club and a positive, me-centered gathering. We come to receive another blessing, another word, another impartation, keys to the kingdom, etc.; however, we do not go back out there to the hurting ones and give away what we have so freely received. We have hoarded all the gifts, impartations, words, revelation, illumination, etc., to ourselves because it makes us feel so good.

I submit to you that we will answer to God for this. The people bound up on drugs needs us to be carriers of the glory in the real way to where they can get relief from their torture. I can imagine that many of them have harsh feelings towards the church because we seem so fake, removed and impartial to their sufferings. I remember when I was homeless on the streets and when it came time to go to church I felt terrible. In my mind I was thinking, "I stink. I have no clean clothes. I cannot fix my hair. All these people coming in with their superfluous lifestyles and I'm hurting. I don't want them to see me like this and I don't want to be around fake people right now. I'm hurting."

However, I went and just laid on my face on the floor most of the time crying out to God in my suffering. No one seemed to care. God did.

Violence on the Rise in our Nation

If people can't see this happening, then they are not paying attention. There is an outbreak of anger and violence in our streets. Not only in the streets with these pre-planned riots held by the left-winged socialist and antichrist groups. Violence is on the rise and the church must consider our role in this as well. First, we should not be voting for organizations like this or participating in evil agendas. We will answer to God for this. The *Women's March* movement, which is a progressive, left-winged agenda (feminist), are the ones behind all the marches taking place having to do with the children right now. It's clearly stated on their website!

As you can see by their pictures, the adults are coordinating this rebellion and walk-outs in the schools. This is a huge coordinated event and Satanic to the core. Their goal is to rally the progressives to run for office and to put the Democrats back in control. However, people cannot see the real agenda taking place. Don't forget that their plan is also to take control of the country in an evil way (we saw that with Obama and Hilary Clinton). We knew that if Hilary were in office we will slide right off a cliff. This group's propaganda is to present to the public that they are in retaliation to Trump winning the election. They marched the day after his inauguration. It's all a setup.

Another form of violence is in the schools. I believe this is a setup as well. I believe that the shootings in Las Vegas and the schools are all diabolically pre-planned and designed to target Christians and white people.

If you've all noticed, the ones getting killed are majority white people.

Also, the killers are white people 90% of the time. The reason I believe this is the case is because the powers that be have an agenda. White people = Christianity. (their agenda).

They are trying to force the government into gun confiscation, taking our rights on the internet (shutting up the conservative voice – Christian voice and conversation), and changing the conversation to keep us distracted and send us into chaos.

The Racial War and Divide

They are working hard to divide the nation and the church racially (black and white) because they want to use the black people's past hurts and anger against modern day Christianity. For years we've heard that they are labeling Christianity to be the white man's religion, and the Islam faith is meant for the black man. They are also pulling the black man into the Hebrew Roots movement. This came through the false Black Liberation Theology doctrine. Many "apostles" now are trying to rid the world of the Holy Bible because a white man published it (King James). Thus…it is racist. There is no race creed or color in the Kingdom of God.

In my research I discovered that many theologians believe that the Islam religion was started by the Catholic Church. It sounds shocking, however, I learned that the opposites are all ran by the same powers-that-be. One example is the Democrats and Republicans. Since Trump has been in office we see that they're alike. According to propaganda, they present it to the world that they both come after him. They try to present it to the world that Trump is in the middle. I submit to you that he is not. He knows exactly what he is doing.

See, it's perfect control when the controllers control both side of the voice. Imagine this as religions.

This is a tactic of the enemy to divide the church and nation. First, I've talked to many black ministers about this. We must go by the word of God over any situation or outward situation. We can't change Christianity based upon circumstances.

God's word never changes. It doesn't matter who the person is that is the offender. The powers that be are wanting to divide the church along racial lines and here is how they are doing it:

Media highlighting and twisting facts about cases of crime on black people. (Not saying Africans because the issue is based on color). Out of all the millions of situations in the world, why do they not show the injustices done to the white people by other races or from the Muslims persecuting Christians? Why? Because of their agenda to divide.

Look at Martin Luther King, Jr. and how he handled the injustices. He was peaceful. We know what happened with Malcolm X's Islam answer to violence. We must preach love and forgiveness if we are Christians; and reconciliation.

When Obama took office, Hollywood immediately switched the bosses to black people to show them in authority. Communications and media is my major, so I notice these trends. I also noticed how in television and movies the black people are the heroes and smart ones while the villains are the white people. It's things like this that shift the nation mindset.

In other words, the nation's views towards white people are negative on TV, movies, college textbooks, lower education textbooks, advertisings, and other cultural things. They're trying to emasculate the white man as well.

They're doing this through all the above and attacking the man's identity through the LGBTQ community and transgender rolls.

"The new movie, Black Panther, is a tool by the enemy to fuel the black church by trying to associate them with the African roots. However, the roots they are displaying in this film is rooted in Witchcraft.

According to this ministry, "The movie Black Panther is breaking massive records at the box office. The black community feels that they are finally represented. But is there more at play? Why all the sudden now does Hollywood want to promote black strength? Most of us aren't asking these questions. Black Panther is a movie serving witchcraft and the occult to the black community as being normal. Most of us don't realize it because we're so caught up with our blackness, we put it before our God. Our blackness is an idol and it prevents us from seeing things clearly." (Truthunedited, 2018)

The devil has used social media to fuel the flames. The powers that be know this power, so they will create videos and memes (pictures with words on top and bottom) to fuel the fire against white people. I'm telling you, there is power in social media.

Now with Maxine Waters speaking at a rally in June 2018 insisting that the Democrats were more holy than the Republicans because they care about the children, she encouraged the country to rebel against any Trump supporter! By her doing this it resulted in riots across the country. This will do nothing but escalate in the days ahead. According to this media, "Sen. Maxine Waters (D-CA) called for attacks against members of President Donald Trump's administration over the weekend, screaming to a group of supporters that they should not be welcomed anywhere in society.

Waters' rage- filled rant reportedly happened "during a toy drive outside the Wilshire Federal Building on Saturday," according to The American Mirror.

Waters, who falsely claimed that Trump was 'sacrificing our children,' appeared intent on inciting violence, saying, 'If you think we're rallying now, you ain't seen nothing yet.'" (Saavedra, 2018)

When we examined the 40-day idols, one of them was social justice. The Lord gave that to me in a dream.

We are not to put tribe, nation (races), or ideology above God. When we think that our skin color is more important than God's word, then it's an idol to us. We must surrender all our hurts and pains to God and trust that He is working them out. He is in control, not us. So, when judgment hits, people that are attached to this idol, God will take it down.

I lost a best friend when Trump won the election. She was so mad, and it cost us our relationship.

I could not understand how a black minister can vote Democrat (especially when the lines were drawn with Hilary on evil vs. good). No matter who was running for president we always had to vote lesser of both evils (usually Republican because they stand more towards the conservative values – biblical values).

So, the line was drawn in the sand between me and her because she went more towards her allegiance to her race and the viewpoint of her world over the word of God versus my allegiance to the word of God over anything. I've always been what they call a value voter. This is someone who votes according to their beliefs (biblical). So, most of my votes are Republican because of this. I have voted Democrat before because the tables were reversed, but 99% of the time it's Republican.

It is sad when most of the black church votes for the antichrist agenda over God's agenda. I believe the lines were drawn on the wheat versus the tares on the 2016 election because God made it very clear to the voters. I believe we will be judged on this.

I had a black minister friend and I noticed this year that she kept posting prejudiced things on her wall. Things like, "You know they only did that because he was black", etc. This was in response to a white cop accused of killing an unarmed black man.

It was things like that posted all the time. How can a minister post such things? It's how this Black Liberation Theology has crept in the church so much. As ministers, we are to be reconciliation of peace. We are to show the world that we are different. We love all people no matter the color and even if injustice is happening, we trust in God, etc. We do not alienate a whole race because of it.

The world is going to be the world. We should not get caught up in the anger, etc.

When I went to Detroit to do the racial healing revival, I ran up against a huge racist spirit! This spirit did NOT want racial healing! The African American community there refused to forgive the white people on television. All we were doing is forgiving one another. I was a southern white woman and she was a northern black woman. She received so much backlash from the others that she backed out right before I went LIVE. God spoke to us that week about what he wanted said and since she refused to do it because of the pressure of the others, God did it anyways through a bunch of strangers who showed up at the revival. These strangers were a bunch of white people. They saw that something was wrong, and they obeyed the Lord and said the very things that the Holy Spirit told us to say that week. So, God accomplished his goal despite that dumb demon! So, I saw first-hand how evil this spirit is.

49

NOTE Now that I've been to Washington and realize how the government and media pits us against each other and how the Republicans and Democrats are all working together, I realize what a tragedy it is for both the whites and blacks. It's a tragedy what happened to my friendship based on the lies that we believed through our culture. They drive the wedge but are all fighting for the same thing in the end.

One side fights against abortion, other agrees with it, but in the end nothing changes…even with a President working with you. He has the authority to sign an executive order to stop it like he did with anti-Semitism for the Jews. He has given many executive orders. How many has he for the evangelicals?

The Homosexual Agenda/Transgender/Gender Identity

The way to measure this agenda is by the media. When you notice the commercials, TV shows, movies, advertisements, textbooks, school agendas, and other educational systems pushing tolerance towards a certain thing, then you know that is their agenda. They will literally hit the public on all sides with this.

We have experienced them shoving the homosexual agenda down our throats for many years. When Obama put the rainbow colors on the White House as a symbolic gesture that the LGBTQ agenda had won the Supreme Court case and can now have legal marriages, we knew judgment was coming to the church. That made many

Christians sick to their stomachs. It was a smack in God's face.

In addition to this atrocity, they are changing the sex of popular television personalities and plastering it up all over television, then you know they are pushing the transgender agenda.

Another example of pushing the agenda to form tolerance and inclusion is like putting this narrative on favored shows such as *The Voice* on NBC. They had a guest on there who was a praise and worship leader during the day (he was black) and a drag-queen at night. The reason I pointed out that he was black is because I believe this reflects the sickness polluting that race by joining this progressive and perverse agenda.

So, this man was up there singing worldly songs in his women's sexy clothes and the pastors of his church in the audience cheering him on! This is gross in God's eyes and a stench in His nostrils. See, Tyler Perry acting funny with Medea personality has encouraged the church that it's okay to dress as a woman and be someone else. Although I have laughed hysterically at Tyler's funny shows, I believe it has opened the door to the young black men who grew up without a father to do this for attention.

Now that we have infiltrated society with the homosexual and transgender agenda, now it is the gender war. This means that you can now identify yourself as a male, female, other, or nothing or as anything you want. Following this catastrophe, the next will be pedophilia and bestiality.

Pedophilia is with children and bestiality is with animals. This is all a stench in God's nostrils and when you vote for associations that agree with all this abomination, then their blood is on your hands as well. You will answer to God for it. God hates us mixing and touching the unclean thing. If you don't know it, the bestiality law is already before the Supreme Court and legal in many countries!

Looking at the area of the LGBTQ infiltration into America, the church must consider our part into this sinful penetration. We have quit loving our neighbors and caring about what Suzie Q next door is going through. In the days of old, it took a village to raise a family.

The whole neighborhood was friends and the kids had many eyes on them. Also, we had relationships with one another. Let's not forget the churches who are now placing people in authority who are perverted and filled with demons of the LGBTQ kind. We are partnering with the world in that we are including this behavior in our own churches.

When pastors are confronted with the exposure of perversion demons being leaders in their praise and worship teams and they do not confront it, then they are opening the door wide to perversion to fill their churches. God hates pollution.

The evangelical church leaders have now partnered with the LGBTQ groups under the guise of President Trump. I exposed a lot of this in 2019. The President partnered with them due to the *Walk Away* agenda. I will explain more later. It is a sure sign of how sick our church is.

Another thing to consider is the battle of one of our biggest denominations in 2019 – the Methodists. Their council voted to abolish all ties to the LGBTQ agenda in February 2019. This meant no more gay preachers, marrying them, or endorsing the movement. There was huge backlash and then in 2020's council, they split. The war over this spirit is real.

The World in the Church – Everywhere

The world has certainly infiltrated the church in America. Statistics show that the divorce rate is just as bad in the church.

Lust is running rampant through TV, music, and now in our churches.

You can tell by the way the people do not seem to respect or reverence God by the way they dress. They come to church with very revealing clothes on, and this includes the men. They come to church and even preach on the platform with skinny jeans. When you wear skinny jeans, it shows the man's "package" in the front and in the back. They are so tight and built for homosexual men.

This is very inappropriate for men. Just imagine if you have a man in the congregation who battles homosexuality or if you have a woman who has a lust demon.

They can be distracted the whole time because you can't get your flesh under control.

We must dress appropriately in church to respect other people and to not be a stumbling block. If you don't believe me Bride, check out a gay men's clothing store online.

See how they are very tight and show all the men's body, to include the new meggings (men's leggings). It's sick and gross.

I saw in a Pentecostal church one time and there was a mother/daughter duo that sat on the front row every service. The daughter was in her young twenties and wore tank tops and very revealing blouses all the time! Her bra size was like an EE or something. Anyways, I just started that church, so I was wondering if anyone has instructed this girl on how inappropriate this was in a church. How terrible for the pastor! So, one day I asked the mother of the church and she said that they confront the mother and daughter all the time and it never stops. She explained how embarrassed they was and didn't know what to do about this new generation. I wondered if the pastor would say anything. I don't imagine he ever did but the family ended up moving away.

This family is not a wicked family. I lived with them for a few months. They were nice enough to open their home up when I was homeless and at the end when it was time for me to leave, the Lord woke me up with a dream and instructions for those two ladies. I don't know why the girl continued to disobey the authorities in the church or even why her mother didn't help to enforce it.

However, it does reflect on our society and the non-confrontation to sin in our leaders now.

Music in the Church

Another way the world has infiltrated the church is through the music. Allowing worldly music in the church is Satanic to the core. The reason is because music is controlled by one spirit or the other.

The influence behind that music is what will be imparted when listened to by the audience. I know this for many reasons. When I was saved in the 80s I watched a documentary called *Hell's Bells – Dangers of Rock and Roll Music*. This documentary greatly explained how music affects us in body, soul and spirit.

I see now how it has even infiltrated in the contemporary Christian music. Setting the Christian music aside, just consider how worldly music has entered the church. Many music ministries will take worldly songs and try to put Christian lyrics to it. God hates mixing. This isn't holy at all. Many churches play Beyoncé's songs and other worldly artists during their services! Sacrilege! Terrible!

As far as the Christian world, I say that music has been the catalyst to the great deception. As renowned musicologist David Tame, "Music is the language of languages. It can be said that of all the arts, there is none more powerfully moves or changes the consciousness." (Garth, 2011)

The enemy has used music to seduce the masses.

We do not realize that although the beat sounds great, the lyrics sound so perfect, that we do not actually pay attention to what they're really saying. Because it just feels so right we do not pay attention. However, it is entering our subconscious and slowly taking us out. According to this documentary, they can hypnotize people and cause them to do what they say.

According to Eddy Manson, "Music is used everywhere to condition the human mind. It can be just as powerful as a drug and much more dangerous, because nobody takes musical manipulation very seriously." (Chadbourne, 2020)

Eddy Manson was internationally known harmonica player and composer of background music for television and motion pictures. Eddy apparently knows what he is talking about! Look what this article says about him on his obituary:

"The prolific composer also scored several television movies, including 'Crash: The True Story of Flight 401,' and for motion pictures presented in theaters, including 'Lovers and Lollipops' in 1956 and 'Three Bites of the Apple' in 1967. Manson's voluminous output included original concert pieces, among them 'Fugue for Woodwinds,' 'Ballad for Brass,' 'Parable for 16 Horns' and 'Yankee Doodle Toccata.' He composed music for several commercials and arranged music for individuals and groups such as Michael Jackson, Don Ho and the Jackson Five. The performer and composer taught film scoring at UCLA and was a columnist for Overture magazine." (Oliver, 1996)

As you can see, this comes from a man who understood the power of music in society. We must pay attention to the lyrics.

There are many watchdog websites out there to identify the false within the church. These people are watchman on the wall. Checkout what *Emergent Watch* says about this music;

Once the enemy gets you in the subjective, sensual, emotional arena, where God's Word is no longer the objective foundation – Then you can be manipulated, being led by seductive sensations and feelings, and discernment become almost impossible.

It has been observed that much of the contemporary Christian music by Hillsong, Bethel and Jesus Culture, etc. has more in common with the songs of the Trance genre, than with genuine Christian worship.

It is no secret that Bethel Redding teaches the doctrinal aberrations of the New Apostolic Reformation [NAR].

Their practices are also deviant – and from "grave sucking" to "fire tunnels" and the shaking and quaking of the Toronto "blessing", etc. – Bethel attendees have been shown exhibiting some of the most bizarre occultic manifestations. This is the ripened fruit of Bethel. Consider what Bethel Music says of itself, that they are: "a worship ministry formed as an extension of Bethel (Redding) Church and founded by Brian and Jenn Johnson". A tree is surely known by its fruit. (Jefferies, 2017)

This watchman ministry describes this well, "The demonic laughing and jerking, waking up angels, fire tunnels, grave sucking, dead-raising teams, using tuning forks for prophecy, gold dust falling in the meetings, so-called drunken glory, etcetera, are in the simmering cauldron that is Bethel Church. Bethel Music will lead many people back to that cauldron. That is its purpose. Bethel Music does not go around the country putting on concerts to showcase talent, to entertain people, or to make lots of money.

The so-called worship team is on the road for one purpose. That purpose is to unite people with the spirits that comprise its source, Bethel Church." (Fisher, 2015)

Bill Johnson believes, "Music bypasses all the intellectual barriers and when the anointing of God is on a song, people will begin to believe things they wouldn't believe through teaching.

- Bill Johnson." (Johnson, Bill Johnson Quotes, 2000)

This statement shows that he knows the power of music to push ideals and beliefs. For right now I'm just exposing you to how Satan is luring people in through the music. Please pay attention to the lyrics and see if they are not doctrine- sound. It's more about feelings and experience.

We must protect all gates. The ear-gate, mouth-gate, eye-gate, hand-gate, sexual-gate, heart-gate, etc. In the 70s it was discovered how some rock and roll music had subliminal messages. This is a known fact. They played some albums backwards and you could hear a subliminal message such as, "worship Satan", etc. (Régimbal, 2015)

Look at what Mick Jagger, famous rocker, said, "Mick Jagger of the Rolling Stones, who calls himself the 'Lucifer of Rock,' states: 'We always strive to direct the thoughts and wills of people and most of the other groups do the same.' In his best-seller Do it! Scenarios of the Revolution, anarchist Jerry Rubin wrote. 'Elvis woke up our bodies, changing them completely. The secret of immoral heavy rock lies in the energetic beat, which intensely penetrates our bodies, that rhythm which makes all passions surge, drowning out everything else. The backseat of a car was the movie theater of the sexual revolution, while the car radio was the medium for this subversion. Rock marked the beginning of the revolution.

We have fused a new political life with a psychedelic lifestyle. Our way of living, our acid, our freaky clothes, our rock music: This is the true revolution." (Régimbal, 2015)

Final Words About The Sickness

After noticing the influx of New Age in the church, the lack of fear of God, the tattoos increasing, the hippie spirit, the lack of the word of God being preached, the false miracles, signs & wonders, and many other things, it's no denying she is sick. I noticed it in the people and the lack of fire when it came to MAGA Revival tour!

It wasn't until I researched the symptoms did I discover what is truth.

This is what birthed the 40 days fasting & prayer. We addressed the forty idols before God each day. I will share that in the next book.

Also, when I was at the UN and saw our evangelical leaders sitting with the other religions knowing what they're up to, I was done. If our leaders are perverted spiritually, then our nation will only reflect it.

Why Expose?
Devil Comes as an Angel of Light

Bride, many are out there teaching that we should not speak truth and expose the false, etc. I do understand that the word says we should not speak EVIL of our brother. We should not BARE FALSE WITNESS against someone. However, to the false prophets it's another ballgame. Let's answer this question by the word of God:

1 Timothy 1:17-20 - 17 Now unto the King eternal, immortal, invisible, the only wise God, be honour and glory for ever and ever. Amen.

18 This charge I commit unto thee, son Timothy, according to the prophecies which went before on thee, that thou by them mightest war a good warfare; 19 Holding faith, and a good conscience; which some having put away concerning faith have made shipwreck: 20 Of whom is Hymenaeus and Alexander; whom I have delivered unto Satan, that they may learn not to blaspheme.

Ephesians 5:11 And have no fellowship with the unfruitful works of darkness, but rather reprove them.

Proverbs 9:6-8 - 6 Forsake the foolish, and live; and go in the way of understanding. 7 He that reproveth a scorner getteth to himself shame: and he that rebuketh a wicked man getteth himself a blot. 8 Reprove not a scorner, lest he hate thee: rebuke a wise man, and he will love thee.

So, as the scripture describes, we must expose so that humanity will see the truth. If no one exposes it, how will they know? The apostles and Jesus exposed all the time.

4

Ecumenical Movement
&
The Catholic Church

The ecumenical movement is a movement to try to bring unity to all the faiths and eventually form the one world religion. The Catholic Church is the group behind it and they control the world basically. They are very powerful and not to be underestimated! After studying eschatology, I am convinced the Catholic Church is the great whore of Babylon that the Bible talks about. This whore gathers all the religions of the Earth together and seduces the masses into this evil plot. They then help to pave the way for the one world government and the Antichrist to sit on the throne. The Antichrist will fool the world and seduce them as well. What is funny is that halfway through the Tribulation, the beast (Antichrist) turns around and kills the great whore! He gets jealous and ousts her! She thinks she's all powerful right now!

The Catholic church is spewing her poison while America partners with her and funds most of it. We also have the connection of the Noahide Laws with Orthodox Jews.

What is the Ecumenical Movement?

As I stated in the Terms and Conditions chapter, it is a group that is forming a one world religion. It taints the church and brings sin it. It is moving her to the left. They call it either "community", "coexist", "universe", "circle", or "Christ-Consciousness". They want everyone to be in this great Utopia and be in peace. The Pope wants everyone to feminize God. You can tell this by his missiology document.

In current days, the Ecumenical Movement's roots are from the Roman Catholic Church and is managed through a division called the World Council of Churches. Through these two, it has branched off into thousands of other networks. This thing is massive in size globally. Please see their graphic from their website: https://www.oikoumene.org/en/wcc70/

In 2018 they celebrated their 70th year celebration. This is also the same year as Israel became a nation. Are you shocked to learn that the UN is the one that created the State of Israel? The globalist are the ones who put the nation back together. Rockefeller helped to fund it. Rockefeller is a Jew. The rabbit trail is so long.

According to their website, "Walking together, serving justice and peace. In 2018 we celebrate the 70th anniversary of the World Council of Churches and the fellowship that is its heart and soul. This is an opportunity to mark the achievements of the past 70 years in working for Christian unity and action, and to look to the challenges ahead as a fellowship of churches responding to God's call for unity, mission, justice and peace." (World Council of Churches, 2018)

It began in 1905 and has had this goal in mind since the beginning. Remember: As Above- So Below.

History of the Ecumenical Movement

Retrieved from The Association of Religion Data Archives – ARDA

(ARDA, 2018) also

The Encyclopedia of Christianity in the United States

- o 1905 - Federal Council of Churches of Christ in America
- o (FCC) met
- o 29 denominations to discuss coming together.
- o Met at Carnegie Hall, New York
- o Wanted to form because of issues surrounding labor, social inequality, urbanism, and poverty
- o 1908 - FCC had 1st huge meeting in Philadelphia.
- o "The Evangelization of the World in This Generation"
- o FCC Became official
- o Met because they were concerned w/social problems.
- o 1910 – World Missionary Conference (WMC)
- o Brought US delegates from different denominations who wanted to evangelize the world
- o Leaders were
- o ☐ John Mott, Nobel Peace Prize winner and American Methodist Pastor
- o ☐ J.H. Oldham – Scottish Free Church
- o 1,200 representatives, largely Anglo-American
- o Theme – "The Evangelization of the World in This Generation"
- o President of WMC is Alexander Bruce and Sixth Lord Balfour of Burleigh
- o Catholics were not invited to this meeting

o 1910 – 1948 – Many Significant Events
o 1911 Conference on Faith & Order
o Included Anglican, Protestant, Roman Catholic, Eastern Orthodox & Others
o ☐ Bishop Charles Brent at Episcopal is Leader
o 1920 Encyclical published by the Eastern Orthodox Patriarch of Constantinople
o "Unto all the Churches of Christ Everywhere"
   o This was unique as a call for unity and cooperation issued by one church to all other churches calling for an end to bitterness, mistrust, and proselytism, as well as beginning to extensive theological dialog and practical cooperative witness.
o This proposed "League of Churches"
o Would come to be embodied in the:
   o Faith & Order Movement
   o Life & Work Movement
o 1925 – Archbishop Nathan Soderblom (1836- 1931) of Sweden
o Conducted 1st Life & Work Conference in Stockholm
o Motto – "Doctrine Divides, Service Unites"
o 1927 – Faith & Order
o Bishop Charles Brent of the Protestant Episcopal Church
   o He had attended the 1910 WMC Mtg & 1911 Mtg and saw need to go beyond just missions & begin dialoging over doctrine & ministry.
   o He suggested the 1st mtg in 1911, but official mtg didn't happen until 1927
o Meeting Held at Lausanne, Switzerland

- 400 participants representing 127 church bodies from Anglican, Protestant, Roman Catholic, and Eastern Orthodox
- All churches "which confess Our Lord
- Jesus Christ as God and Savior"
- ☐ Catholics vs. Protestants clashed over The Nicene Creed
- 1937 - Life & Work Mission
- ☐ 610 official representatives to include Catholics
- ☐ Problem became over deciding how to build the "Kingdom of God on Earth" for social transformation
- Held in Oxford, England
- 1937 - Life & Work plus Life & Order decided to combine to form World Council of Churches (WCC), but had to delay because of WWII
- 1948 – World Council of Churches (WCC) officially formed
- Same year as Israel became a nation
- Held in Amsterdam
- 44 Nationalities Representatives from 147 churches
- Roman Catholic Church declined to participate
- Gives freedom for ministries to continue in their own doctrine & teachings
  - 1950 – FCC changed name to National Council of Church of Christ (NCC)
- Presently has 37 denominations including Roman Catholic, Southern Baptist, Lutheran & others
  - 1961 & 1971 – WCC merged with International Missionary Council and World Council of Christian Education

- o 1962 – Consultation on Church Union (COCU) Started
- o Truly Catholic, Truly Evangelical, & Truly Reformed
  - o 1962 – 2nd Vatican Council
- o Frère Max Thurian was invited by the Pope Paul VI to participate in the liturgical reform of the Catholic Mass.
- o Birth of Taizé Community – an ecumenical place
- o Discussed opening up MASS to Protestants
- o Addressed relations between the Catholic Church and the modern world
- o 2nd to be held at St. Peter's Basilica in the Vatican
  - o 1965 – Joint Catholic-Orthodox Declaration
  - o 1974 – Lausanne Movement Congress Mtg
- o Leader was Billy Graham & John Stott
- o This formed the Lausanne Covenant
  - o 1982 – Faith & Order Plenary Meeting
- o Lima, Peru
- o Panel of Theologians
- o Created the Baptism, Eucharist, and Ministry (BEM) document
- o An agreement between Catholics & Protestants
- o BEM has been a basis for many "mutual recognition" agreements among churches and remains a reference today

These are highlights from this BEM document!

• So, it is that the stated aim of the Commission is "to proclaim the oneness of the Church of Jesus Christ and to call the churches to the goal of visible unity in one faith and one eucharistic fellowship, expressed in worship and common life in Christ, in order that the world might believe" (By-Laws).

• If the divided churches are to achieve the visible unity they seek, one of the essential prerequisites is that they should be in basic agreement on baptism, eucharist and ministry.

• As the churches grow into unity, they are asking how their understandings and practices of baptism, eucharist and ministry relate to their mission in and for the renewal of human community as they seek to promote justice, peace and reconciliation. Therefore, our understanding of these cannot be divorced from the redemptive and liberating mission of Christ through the churches in the modern world.

• Indeed, because of biblical and patristic studies, together with the liturgical revival and the need for common witness, an ecumenical fellowship has come into being which often cuts across confessional boundaries and within which former differences are now seen in a new light.

• In the process of growing together in mutual trust, the churches must develop these doctrinal convergences step by step, until they are finally able to declare together that they are living in communion with one another in continuity with the apostles and the teachings of the universal Church.

• We believe that the Holy Spirit has led us to this time, a Kairos of the ecumenical movement

• The suggestions your church can make for the ongoing work of Faith and Order as it relates the material of this text on Baptism, Eucharist and Ministry to its long-range research project "Towards the Common Expression of the Apostolic Faith Today".

Continuing History Timeline

• 1989 – NCC made NRS Bible – New Revised Standard

• 1999 – COCU Fell apart

• 1999 - Joint Declaration on the Doctrine of Justification

o representatives of the Lutheran World Federation and the Roman Catholic Church concluded two decades of dialogue

• 2002 – COCU came back to Churches Uniting in Christ (CUIC) @ Memphis where Martin Luther King, Jr. was assassinated

o Met there for commitment to counteracting racism

o African Methodist Episcopal Church, Disciples of

Christ, Christian Methodist Episcopal Church, Episcopal Church, International Council of Community Churches, Moravian Church (Northern Province), Presbyterian Church (USA), United Church of Christ, and United Methodist Church. The Evangelical Lutheran Church in America is a partner as well for mission & dialogue.

• 2013 – WCC Missions Conference

• 2018 – WCC Conference on World Mission and Evangelism

Highlights from 2018 Conference

A New Reformation: Evangelism as Life Together Jin S. Kim

• According to the Second Vatican Council, Protestants are not part of the true church but are to be considered "separated brethren" – in other words, family, but homeless.

Thankfully, most Catholics and Protestants today seem to agree that we are at least separated brethren, if not all "real" Christians. But this détente may be too little, too late. The logic of distrust, recrimination, schism and endless splintering seems to be part of the DNA of the institutional church, and this logic is passed on like an infection to the faithful of every ecclesiastical tribe. More and more people are giving up on the church altogether. Who needs one more place of isolation and fracturedness in their lives?

• Every few months at Church of All Nations (CAN), we offer a class for visitors who want to become members of our congregation, and by extension, of the church catholic.

• Today, we see growing impatience with the institutional church's accommodation to temporal power. Younger generations, no longer willing to give the church the benefit of the doubt, are driving the mass exodus out of the Western church, which they see as a primary source of pain and abuse in the world. But for those who have not given up on the church as a vessel of God's grace and transformation, the contours of a new reformation are beginning to surface.

• The church has certainly been a force for good in countless ways, and it is right for Christians to celebrate that heritage. But an honest accounting also requires us to admit that for most of its history the institutional church has in alternating ways been both the master and servant of Western empires. Is there another way? Can modern disciples truly follow the way of Jesus over the American way?

• A New Generation - The church continues only as the next generation accepts the call to be Christ's body, and his hands and feet to the world.

As a pastor in a mainline church for twenty-five years, I have noted the dwindling numbers of young people in the local church. The children of Boomers see the church today as complicit in, and co- opted by, the ways of the world. They have little interest in perpetuating the Constantinian arrangement in which churches produce loyal foot soldiers for the empire du jour.

• The Protestant Reformation and the Radical Reformation were supposed to inaugurate a new era of integrity and faithfulness for the church. But today we see that whether a congregation is Lutheran, Methodist, Baptist, Quaker, Mennonite, or Presbyterian (like ours), that they are overwhelmingly white, old, and declining. Such is the fruit of the Reformation after 500 years.

• Basically, saying that the current church system is not satisfying the people anymore, so they want this: "Our young people desire authentic faith. They are prone to agnosticism or even raw atheism as they see little evidence of a God that makes a difference in the religious institutions of the day, namely the local church."

• We firmly believe that, after 500 years, the Protestant Reformation is giving way to another tectonic shift in what it means to be church. A new reformation is coming indeed.

• One element of that reformation will be learning to live together in intentional Christian community. Living out the Acts 2 way of being church, of sharing all things in common in an age of individualism, greed, loneliness and despair.

• Christians are to be called out of a sick society built on the evils of racism, sexism, militarism, exploitation, ecocide and destructive competition. We are to create a new community of love.

• Rather, we seek to pool our people's resources, talents, ideas, and labor for the common good. We want our members to feel that their work is rewarding, that the fruit of their labor is being shared justly, that they work together, live together, play together, and pray together because it is very good and pleasant when kindred live together in unity. We will have to participate in the broader economic system, but we will not allow capitalist dogma to influence our internal economics.

• We will draw people from our immediate context of great brokenness, but our mission will include the casting out of imperial demons and the healing of bodies and souls so that we can relate rightly to our God, our neighbors (human and non-human), and God's good green earth.

• We aspire to create an urban village founded on the love and teachings of Jesus Christ our Lord, to live life together, and to share God's abundance with an impoverished world.

• Is this part of the next Reformation, or just a pipe dream? We're not sure, but we pray that Christians can live together in harmony as a counter witness to a world falling apart.

My Thoughts

Bride, there is so much I could say about this document. First, they're speaking code. I recognize it so here's my interpretation. First, he's saying that the world is tired of the white old traditional western church. We are what stands in the way of their Utopia.

They want to build this "community" of love and bliss. You will see throughout this book that this document is confirming what I put in this book.

71

Current Day Mission

This organization works hard to bring unity among all faiths. Their mission says, "It is a community of churches on the way to visible unity in one faith and one eucharistic fellowship, expressed in worship and in common life in Christ.

It seeks to advance towards this unity, as Jesus prayed for his followers, so that the world may believe." (John 17:21) (World Council of Churches, 2018)

However, in Roger Oakland's theory, he says that the Pope is forming this ecumenical dialogue to return all back to the Catholic Church and to do a worldwide mission to bring the world to the Eucharist Jesus. He describes this Eucharist Jesus as a false one based upon transubstantiation.

This is when the Catholics take communion and they literally believe that the bread (Eucharist) is literally Jesus in the flesh and the wine both are not substitutes like we say (Protestants)…but Jesus reincarnated. (Oakland, Another Jesus? The Eucharistic Christ and the New Evangelization, 2004). The bread is put in a device called a monstrance and it displays the wafer and the Catholics worship it as if it was Jesus. They literally believe it is him inside this monstrance. Please see the picture. In the middle of the circle is the wafer (Wikipedia Contributors, 2020)

WCC States their goal as the following:

For its member churches, the WCC is a unique space: one in which they can reflect, speak, act, worship and work together, challenge and support each other, share and debate with each other. As members of this fellowship, WCC member churches:

• are called to the goal of visible unity in one faith and one eucharistic fellowship;

• promote their common witness in work for mission and evangelism;

• engage in Christian service by serving human need, breaking down barriers between people, seeking justice and peace, and upholding the integrity of creation; and

• foster renewal in unity, worship, mission and service. (World Council of Churches, 2018)

Through my research I have discovered that this is all satanic to the core because God hates mixing. If this organization wants to mix all religions together under a false Jesus, then God has nothing to do with it. Please see the following scriptures on God's heart towards mixing with Egypt (other worldly religions):

> *2 Corinthians 6:14 - Be ye not unequally yoked together with unbelievers: for what fellowship hath righteousness with unrighteousness? and what communion hath light with darkness?*

> *Deuteronomy 7:1-4 - 1 When the LORD thy God shall bring thee into the land whither thou goest to possess it, and hath cast out many nations before thee, the Hittites, and the Girgashites, and the Amorites, and the Canaanites, and the Perizzites, and the Hivites, and the Jebusites, seven nations greater and mightier than thou; 2 And when the LORD thy God shall deliver them before thee; thou shalt smite them, [and] utterly destroy them; thou shalt make no covenant with them, nor shew mercy unto them:*

3 Neither shalt thou make marriages with them; thy daughter thou shalt not give unto his son, nor his daughter shalt thou take unto thy son.

Romans 16:17 - Now I beseech you, brethren, mark them which cause divisions and offences contrary to the doctrine which ye have learned; and avoid them.

1 Corinthians 5:11 - But now I have written unto you not to keep company, if any man that is called a brother be a fornicator, or covetous, or an idolater, or a railer, or a drunkard, or an extortioner; with such an one no not to eat.

Psalms 26:4 - I have not sat with vain persons, neither will I go in with dissemblers.

Deuteronomy 7:2 - And when the LORD thy God shall deliver them before thee; thou shalt smite them, and utterly destroy them; thou shalt make no covenant with them, nor shew mercy unto them:

There are so many other scriptures. If you study the Torah (first five books in the Old Testament), then you will learn God's heart about touching the unclean thing.

God shows us example after example of how He wants us set apart and not to mix our beliefs or actions with other faiths. He is jealous for us so why would He want us striving for more than just Him? It makes no sense.

So, the ecumenical movement began to bring people together to basically come back to the home church (mother church, Catholic Church). They explain it right on their website.

How They Convince People to Join Ecumenical Movement

Their main pull is social justice. They try to convince all these faiths that when we come together in unity and fight for the "common good" of mankind, then we help the Earth. They also say that it's Jesus' will that they all be in unity in the faith. This is deceiving because there is a much sinister motive. My job in this book is not to convince you of all their tactics and motives, but to merely show you the big picture of what they are doing and how not to get involved in the great deception. You can research more by simply Googling the term "ecumenical movement", "ecumenism", "one world religion", "new apostolic reformation", and "emergent church". This book is merely to point you in the right direction and to cause you to have your eyes opened to the truth. May God help you on your journey to truth.

On the WCC website it states as well

The WCC 10th Assembly called the churches to join a pilgrimage of justice and peace. This call sets the direction for the WCC in the coming years. All WCC programmes aim to support the member churches and ecumenical partners to journey together, promoting justice and peace in our world as an expression of faith in the Triune God. Today the WCC focuses its work in three programme areas: Unity, Mission, and Ecumenical Relations, Public Witness and Diakonia, and Ecumenical Formation.

All programmes share a responsibility for strengthening relationships with member churches and ecumenical partners, spiritual life, youth engagement, inter- religious dialogue and cooperation and building a just community of women and men. (World Council of Churches WCC, 2018)

This website also explains how they have a missionary school where they want to train up many missionaries to accomplish their world-takeover goals. This school is called GETI (Global Ecumenical Theological Institute), and it's usually held in Jerusalem. Isn't that ironic as well?

Here is what they say about this school, "GETI 2018 is designed for approximately 120 advanced students in theology and related academic fields with an interest in gaining insights into the ecumenical movement's current debates on understanding and practising mission in various regions of the world. GETI 2018 is engaging with the Conference on World Mission and Evangelism's theme, 'Moving in the Spirit: Called to Transforming Discipleship.' The student participants will explore together how the gospel is translated into their different cultures and contexts, and the ways in which they feel called and moved by the Spirit to transform the world. The reflection thereon will be part of a blended study process, which will commence with an e-learning phase a couple of months prior to the event, allowing the students to become familiar with each other and with the purpose and subjects of the programme." (World Council of Churches WCC, 2018)

Another aspect of why to join is the power, network, money acceptance and open doors.

Ecumenical Movement & The Charismatic Church

The part I've studied extensively is on the involvement in the charismatic church. The charismatic church is who I am. It is the Pentecostal section of the Protestants who believe in the gifts of the Holy Spirit and the manifestations of them. When I researched this, I was so shocked to discover who all was in this!

Research it yourself! Just type in a minister's name + ecumenical. It will show you. Almost every big-named preacher that you know of on TV is in this thing. Certainly, the biggest names are, and it's not disputed at all. It is so obvious.

According to Berean Call:

THE SEND'S LOU ENGLE BLESSES THOSE HELPING THE "EVANGELICAL AND CATHOLIC WORLDS BECOME ONE"

For some time now Catholic evangelists Keith and Iwona Major have worked with The Send founder Lou Engle and IHOPKC's (International House of Prayer Kansas City) Mike Bickle to unify Catholics and Protestants.

Lou Engle states, "Keith and Iwona Major are a bridge to helping the Evangelical and Catholic worlds become one. I bless this couple for all they are doing." [1] (emphasis added) This was reason enough to avoid The Send conference (February 2019), and any other spiritual endeavor cobbled together by Engle. Many of those scheduled to speak or perform at The Send also seem oblivious to the difference between Catholic and Christian theology.

For the third time Catholics participated in in the International House of Prayer's Onething conference, held Dec. 28-31, 2018. [2]

In 2015, speaking with Keith Major, leader of that year's Onething Catholic Ecumenical Track, IHOPKC founder Mike Bickle stated: "Well we have so much to learn from all over the Body of Christ—Catholics, charismatics, non-charismatics, denominations, anyone who loves Jesus.

That's why we're hosting an ecumenical track, or actually you're the one leading it, and I so appreciate you doing that, because if you love Jesus and the Word of God, man, we're going on the same direction before the Lord, and we love that. Thank you. (Berean Call, 2019)

You heard it from both of those leaders. They do not deny being ecumenical. Ecumenical is not a good thing. It is terrible. It is mixing. I had a minister get mad at me and say, "What's wrong with Catholics and Christians coming together as one? They're both Christians." This is the key. Do you believe they are true Christians? Do you believe that the Vatican is true? Does it represent Jesus and his covenant today? If so, what about all the idols? The masonic symbolism? The Eucharist? No. God does not approve of that.

Thanks to Kenneth Copeland, the thesis of Martin Luther no longer exists. He is another pawn being used for the ecumenical movement. It is sad because he is the father of the faith movement.

The Lausanne Movement Ecumenical Document
Billy Graham Founder
Signed by World Leaders in 1974

One of the great hallmarks of the Lausanne Movement is its desire to transcend issues which have divided the church and find our deeper unity in the core Gospel message.

The Lausanne Movement is simultaneously an evangelical movement as well as a profoundly ecumenical one.

As part of the ecumenical movement, Lausanne stands in the tradition of the World Evangelical Alliance and the World Council of Churches, but Lausanne has flourished, in part, because it is a movement rather than an organization per se. (Tennent, 2014)

From the Gospel Coalition website about this ecumenical meeting, "2500 evangelicals from 150 countries and 135 denominations were in Lausanne, Switzerland for the International Congress on World Evangelization." (Wax, 2013)

SINCE BILLY GRAHAM FOUNDED IT, I'M INSERTING SOME OF HIS FAMOUS SPEECH DELIVERED AT THE FIRST CONGRESS IN 1974. THIS IS KEY TO US TODAY ABOUT THE ECUMENICAL MOVEMENT.

Why Lausanne? by Billy Graham

'Why Lausanne' is Billy Graham's opening plenary address, given at the First International Congress on World Evangelization in Lausanne, Switzerland, in 1974.

• Since we met in Berlin eight years ago, tremendous developments have been taking place in the religious world. We are all aware of the startling changes in the Roman Catholic world. I also detect a wistful longing on the part of a small but growing number of ecumenical leaders for a greater emphasis on orthodox biblical theology and a re-evaluation of some of the pronouncements in theological, sociological, and political areas.

• One of those important conferences was convened in New York in 1900. At that conference, John R. Mott, who has been called the architect of the ecumenical movement, saw in the command of Christ the responsibility of each generation to preach Christ to its own known and accessible world. The spoken message was to be supported by education, literacy programs, and medicine.

'The goal of the church', he said, 'was the conversion of souls and the edification of the infant churches'. Ten years later, the most historic conference on evangelism and missions of this century was held in Edinburgh, Scotland. But something happened after Edinburgh in 1910.

• It was only a small cloud on the horizon, but it became a cyclone that swept the world. Even before Edinburgh, theological changes were subtly infiltrating Christian youth movements, causing some to weaken their ties to orthodox faith. The authority of evangelism began to shift from the Scriptures to the organized church. They focused attention on the materialistic salvation of the community rather than the individual. This became known as the 'social gospel'. Emphasis turned to man 'in this world', rather than 'in this and the next world'. It is my hope and prayer that Lausanne 1974 will take us back theologically, though not politically or sociologically, to the visions and concepts of those great conferences in the early part of this century. Since then, the world church has floundered. It has lost much of the vision and zeal of those days, for three primary reasons: The loss of the authority of the message of the gospel. The preoccupation with social and political problems. The equal preoccupation with organizational unity. From Edinburgh came two major streams of the modern missionary movement. The first was the evangelical. A second stream might be termed the ecumenical.

• Thus, the spotlight gradually shifted from evangelism to social and political action. Finally, guidelines were drawn up which called almost entirely for humanization—the reconciliation of man with man, rather than of man with God. (Graham, 1974)

I highlighted all the references that I wanted you to pay special attention that were ecumenical in nature. Basically, Billy Graham was informing the congress of the unifying & solidifying the evangelical church in this movement.

He mentioned a fellow named Stott. Stott represented the left side of the Ecumenical Movement. He had a huge presence in London. Well, apparently, he was there at this congress and didn't think Billy Graham was progressive enough with his words and he was not satisfied with the road they were headed down in this document, so he threatened to pull out. The people recorded it as the following, "In the end, they locked Stott and Peter Wagner, a Fuller Seminary professor who wanted Lausanne to focus on strategies for evangelism, in a room and told them to come up with a compromise." (Wax, 2013)

As you can tell by the name of the person to represent Graham and come up with a solution is NOT Billy Graham, but rather the HEAD OF THE NEW APOSTOLIC REFORMATION GUY, Peter Wagner! Isn't that a coincidence? Hmmm. He happened to be at this world conference and the head next to Billy Graham. Wow. He had enough authority that whatever they decided was the final word globally. They ended up coming up with a compromise and that was all that I showed you earlier.

The snowball continues to get bigger!

Now that it is finished, look what the website says about this Covenant, "The Lausanne Covenant, drafted by an international committee chaired by John Stott, has come to be regarded as one of the most significant documents in modern church history. It defined the necessity and goals of evangelism, bringing together evangelicals from diverse backgrounds and shaping much of their endeavors for the rest of the century." (Lausanne.org, 2018)

Even the International Council of Apostolic Leaders Adopt It!

HERE THEY'RE SAYING THAT PEOPLE NEED TO BE RETAUGHT SO THAT THEY ARE MORE CULTURALLY-ACCEPTED AND MORE TOLERANT

Yet we are committed to indigenous principles, and long that every church will have national leaders who manifest a Christian style of leadership in terms not of domination but of service. We recognise that there is a great need to improve theological education, especially for church leaders. In every nation and culture there should be an effective training programme for pastors and laity in doctrine, discipleship, evangelism, nurture and service.

Such training programmes should not rely on any stereotyped methodology but should be developed by creative local initiatives according to biblical standards. (ICAL, 2018)

HERE THEY ARE SAYING THAT NO BELIEF IS HIGHER THAN ANOTHER (PENTECOSTAL BETTER THAN CATHOLIC PERSAY) ....

The gospel does not presuppose the superiority of any culture to another but evaluates all cultures according to its own criteria of truth and righteousness and insists on moral absolutes in every culture. Missions have all too frequently exported with the gospel an alien culture and churches have sometimes been in bondage to culture rather than to Scripture.

Christ's evangelists must humbly seek to empty themselves of all but their personal authenticity to become the servants of others, and churches must seek to transform and enrich culture, all for the glory of God. (ICAL, 2018)

THIS IS DEFINITELY WRITTEN BY CATHOLICS! THEY ARE PROMOTING SOCIALISM!

All of us are shocked by the poverty of millions and disturbed by the injustices which cause it. Those of us who live in affluent circumstances accept our duty to develop a simple life-style in order to contribute more generously to both relief and evangelism. (ICAL, 2018)

HERE THEY ARE PUTTING DOWN THE USA FOR OUR MISSIONS IN THE PAST. SEE, WE ARE KNOWN FOR BEING THE #1 MISSIONS COUNTRY IN THE WORLD, MAINLY OUR PROTESTANT CHURCHES!

We rejoice that a new missionary era has dawned. The dominant role of western missions is fast disappearing. (ICAL, 2018)

HERE THEY ARE SAYING THAT THEY WANT TO REEDUCATE THE CHURCH, PUBLISH NEW BOOKS, TAKE OVER THE MEDIA, AND REIMAGINE A NEW WORLD WHERE THE CATHOLIC CHURCH IS THE HEAD.

A reevaluation of our missionary responsibility and role should be continuous.

Thus a growing partnership of churches will develop and the universal character of Christ's Church will be more clearly exhibited. We also thank God for agencies which labor in Bible translation, theological education, the mass media, Christian literature, evangelism, missions, church renewal and other specialist fields. They too should engage in constant self- examination to evaluate their effectiveness as part of the Church's mission. (ICAL, 2018)

ALL CHURCHES WILL BE UNIFIED UNDERNEATH THE CATHOLIC CHURCH. IF YOU DON'T BELIEVE ME, LOOK AT THE ICAL WEBSITE ON THE STATEMENT OF FAITH PAGE AND SEE THE NICENE CREED AND THE APOSTLE'S CREED WHERE THEY BOTH GIVE LOYALTY TO THE CATHOLIC CHURCH.
THIS IS ALSO ON OTHER BIG-NAMED PREACHER'S WEBSITE ON BELIEFS AS WELL.

The Ecumenical media Christianitytoday.com website has an EM answer to why this is all OK to partner with these creeds:

Protestants, of course, do not equate "catholic" with "Roman Catholic." To avoid this misunderstanding, some prefer to say "holy Christian church." While there is nothing wrong with this term, we should not be embarrassed by the older wording. The word catholic simply means "general, universal, concerning the whole." Jesus prayed that his disciples would be one, even as he and the Father are one, so that the world might believe.

I think it is right to pray and work for the "full visible unity" of Christ's church on Earth which we know for sure will be completely realized when Jesus comes again.

When we say that we "believe in the holy catholic church," we are confessing that Jesus Christ himself is the church's one foundation, that all who truly trust in him as Savior and Lord are by God's grace members of this church, and that the gates of hell shall never prevail against it.

The "communion of saints" is another term from the Apostles' Creed that troubles some Protestants.

"Saints" in the New Testament refers to baptized believers in a local congregation, such as the saints at Corinth, or Ephesus, or Colossae. Some of these believers were far from saintly in their behavior, but they were holy by virtue of their participation (communio) in Christ. The New Testament also recognizes "a great cloud of witnesses" made up of men and women of faith who surround us as we walk the path of faith. Each community within the Christian tradition has its own "saints" in this sense. (George, 2008)

I certainly disagree with this gentleman. There is no way I'm declaring my loyalty to a Catholic church. My only loyalty is to Jesus Christ. I do not see how they can justify the following:

NICENE CREED:

We believe in one God the Father Almighty, Maker of heaven and Earth, and of all things visible and invisible.

And in one Lord Jesus Christ, the only-begotten Son of God, begotten of the Father before all worlds, God of God, Light of Light, Very God of Very God.

Begotten, not made, being of one substance with the Father by whom all things were made; who for us men, and for our salvation, came down from heaven, and was incarnate by the Holy Spirit of the Virgin Mary, and was made man, and was crucified also for us under Pontius Pilate. He suffered and was buried, and the third day he rose again according to the Scriptures, and ascended into heaven, and sitteth on the right hand of the Father.

And he shall come again with glory to judge both the quick and the dead, whose kingdom shall have no end.

And we believe in the Holy Spirit, the Lord and Giver of Life, who proceedeth from the Father and the Son, who with the Father and the Son together is worshipped and glorified, who spoke by the prophets. **And we believe one holy catholic and apostolic Church**. We acknowledge one baptism for the remission of sins. And we look for the resurrection of the dead, and the life of the world to come. Amen.

APOSTLE'S CREED:

I believe in God, the Father Almighty, the Maker of heaven and Earth, and in Jesus Christ, His only Son, our Lord:

Who was conceived by the Holy Ghost, born of the virgin Mary, suffered under Pontius Pilate, was crucified, dead, and buried; He descended into hell.

The third day He arose again from the dead; He ascended into heaven, and sitteth on the right hand of God the Father Almighty; from thence he shall come to judge the quick and the dead.

I believe in the Holy Ghost; the holy catholic church; the communion of saints; the forgiveness of sins; the resurrection of the body; and the life everlasting.

We confess that our testimony has sometimes been marred by a sinful individualism and needless duplication. (ICAL, 2018)

THE CATHOLIC CHURCH HATES INDIVIDUALISM. THEY WANT UNIVERSALISM. THEY ALSO HATE FUNDAMENTALISTS (PEOPLE THAT BELIEVE IN THE TRUE WORD OF GOD LITERALLY – LIKE ME). SEE WHAT THIS COVENANT REQUIRES OF THE PARTICIPANTS (WHICH INCLUDES ICAL). WHEN IT SAYS "NEEDLESS DUPLICATION" THAT MEANS CONVERSIONS. (FROM CATHOLIC TO PROTESTANT).

THEY ARE MAKING THESE PEOPLE AGREE THAT WE HAVE BEEN IN ERROR FOR DOING THAT! THESE ARE PENTECOSTAL APOSTLES AGREEING TO THIS HERESY?

So, Bride, as you can see, The Lausanne Covenant is behind all of this. Are you as shocked as I am that Billy Graham started this? You know who's behind this? The Worldwide Council of Churches. You know who's behind that? The Pope & The Vatican. You know who's behind that? Satan. This is the Great Whore!

Martyrdom by the Catholic Church

According to the following author, the Catholic Church is the Great Whore in Revelation 18. This Great Whore is blood-thirsty after the saints and will eventually kill us all.

The Catholic Church is devising this master plan to take over the world through this Ecumenical Movement (which is basically a lie and a trickery to the Protestants).

It will turn around and attempt to destroy the remaining Bride.

According to the Foxe's Book of Martyrs, "As in France, they have commenced their attacks upon the bible, the Sabbath, marriage, and all the social and domestic relations of life. With flatteries and lies, they are attempting to sow the seeds of discontent and future rebellion among the people.

The ferocity of their attacks upon those who differ from them, even while restrained by public opinion, shews what they would do, provided they could pull down our institutions and Fox's Book of Martyrs, by John Foxe 8 introduce disorder and wild misrule. (Foxe, 2018)

If you get a chance to read that whole article on the Foxe's Book of Martyrs, the link will be in the back of this book. It talks about how the Catholic Church is behind martyring Christians.

It is known throughout history about the Catholic Church trying to control the world and killing people to achieve their mission.

I submit to you Bride that the Catholic Church is behind this global church and will end up killing the "fundamental" Christians. They do not want people who believe in individualism with God.

They want the church to be one good global church or "community". If you are not a part of that you will be killed. They are partnering with the Orthodox Jews as well for Noahide Laws.

If you research the various ways they killed people in the past it's gross. I will also give you the story of an ex-nun who escaped the convents and converted to Pentecostalism. She explained how all this works within the Catholic faith. When she escaped she talked about how her dad brought the priest to come see her.

When she would not renounce this new faith, (recant), he began speaking curses over her.

I submit to you Bride that in the end when they martyr the church, they will say that to us. "You must recant your loyalty to your Christian faith, Jesus Christ, or the OLD ORDER!" Remember they are trying to do away with Christians and Christianity and make us look bad. They're hitting us on every side, through the media, television shows, churches that are EM, etc. They are truly painting us in a bad light on all social media channels.

Interesting Note About EM & The Word "Christ"

Bride, if you will notice when you begin to search all this out is how they continually use the word Christ instead of Jesus Christ or just plain Jesus. I knew something was weird about it because if you only say Christ and not the name Jesus, then you may not be talking about the same Jesus. I found a video of Rob Bell speaking and he's talking to an audience about "Everything is Spiritual".

Listen to this, "Is there a new layer in the universe that has yet to unfold that will only unfold when we bond with each other in similar essence and substance? Is that the next forward movement of the universe?

Are you and I invited to form something that the universe has never seen? Is this why terrorism, racism, inequality, grieve you so deeply? It isn't just individual events, it's like something is trying to rise here and something holding it back. Here's why I find it fascinating, if you read the ancient sages, mystics, and apostles, I think that you can argue that for thousands of years people have been speaking to this.

For example; in the tradition where I come from, the New Testament writers kept speaking of Jesus the Christ.

Now, when they said the Christ, they kept referring to a universal animating energy that holds the whole universe together." (Bell, 2016)

He continues to explain how all the books agree on the same topic. His point is that the kingdom is for one humanity of Christ Consciousness. He explains that their all one body but to an ultimate goal. He then explains the Eucharist.

Rob Bell Explains the Eucharist
Transcribed from YouTube Message –
"Rob Bell / Everything is Spiritual (2016 Tour Film)"

There's a passage in the New Testament this is Christ holds all things together.

They kept speaking of an energy they brought everything into being. It was there in the beginning and they keep speaking of some form of energy at work in the universe pulling everything forward since the beginning.

And they kept speaking of this Christ consciousness in a very particular way. They insisted that we human beings make up a body.

Now why is this interesting?

Well atoms bond with other atoms to create molecules. Molecules have new qualities and characteristics. But we know at least that the molecules have the properties of the Atoms. Make sense? Each new layer has at least the properties of the layer before it.

So based on the pattern that we know of unfolding for 13 billion years, whatever it is that we make up together, would at least have the properties and characteristics of the earlier layer which is personhood and personality.

So whatever it is that we all make-up together, It will at least have some sort of communal personhood and personality. What the ancient mystics kept insisting is that humanity forms one body.

They kept insisting you are all part of one universal human body. Each person has a role to play.

Actually what is really interesting is that there's a 2000-year-old ritual called the Eucharist In which you would gather together with other people. They even had a phrase - they called it "The New Humanity". New Testament phrase - There is a new humanity emerging and the defining characteristic of the new humanity is that Jews and Greeks man and woman it was all sorts of people across all cultures that would never ever associate with each other were coming to gather around a table because they realized that there is a common humanity that we share that trumps any of the ways that we have cooked up to divide ourselves.

There is something that unites us; that more basic to our humanity than any way we could possibly cook up to divide ourselves. And they kept insisting that there was an emerging body of humanity. They called it the body of Christ.

They had a ritual with bread and wine and the idea behind the ritual is called Eucharist; Mass, Agape Supper, communion. The idea behind the ritual is that you will take the bread and wine together.

First off, before you took the bread and wine you would go around and you have make sure that all the single moms had the rent paid. Because we begin by taking care of each other.

We take the bread and wine to heighten our senses to our bonds with our brothers and sisters in our shared humanity.

The meal, first and foremost, wasn't because God was less grumpy because of Jesus.

The atonement theory in 17 seconds, and much more. We are in this together.

There is a new way to be human that's emerging. They even spoke of something being incomplete brought to completion.

Thousands of years ago you had mystics, sages and apostles saying something. There is something new entering into the universe. And it is trying to merge and it is involved all people from all different backgrounds coming to see that there is a new humanity. A common brotherhood and sisterhood that we all share and we embrace each other like this. And something new arises in our midst. (Bell, 2016)

I wanted this documented because this is coming from a man who is ecumenical to the core. He is literally describing the Pope's purpose for the unity!

He wants us to come back to Rome and worship the Eucharist. I will explain more about this later from other sources. I also see the similarities in the way that Bell conducts this speech by trying to make the traditions of the Catholic Church seem hip and cool now. Guess who else is doing that? Kanye!

Dean Odle writes about his discovery of Rob Bell's heresy, "I listened as he taught Yoga to his ten thousand member church and encouraged them to sit at the feet of a total New Ager named Ken Wilber for three months....Sadly Rob Bell has infiltrated the church with false doctrine and most Christians are oblivious to it because he quotes the Bible." (Odle, The Polluted Church; From Rome to Kansas City, 2012)

Ex-Nun Explains Apostasy in Catholic Church

Listen as the words from an ex-nun wrote in her autobiography about going to a cloistered convent, "To become a Bride for Christ was to enjoy bliss of the highest order! To be married in this world might bring disaster and possible deprivation of many necessities. Furthermore, to suffer penance for the lost and dying would not only result in joy and blessings in this life, but eternal bliss and a throne in Heaven." (Keckler, 1999)

See how they called her the "Bride of Christ", but their interpretation must be Christ universal.

This is like the previous false prophet explained. If you read this woman's life story of being tortured as nun in the convent, you will understand how sick that religion is.

The priests would visit the convent once a month and have sex with the nuns. Then their forms of torture were horrible.

She explains how she went to a convent, Sisters of the Open Order. Sounds masonic to me.

Anyways, she explains how she experienced Satanic ritual abuse. As you listen to this testimony I'd like you to consider how that may be future Christians. The Catholics have tortured people in horrible ways in history.

Also, notice the word "bliss". This is a term used a lot in New Age. I explained to you that this one world religion is all New Age. It will include all religions but be from a New Age point. They are working towards a Christ-Consciousness. This means universal consciousness. Unity of the world – Kingdom.

Also, in this story of the nun, they did not read Bibles. In her own words, look who she prayed to, "I turned shamefaced and tiptoed back to my cell and knelt on my prayer board and poured out my tears to my Patron Saint and the Virgin Mary." (Keckler, 1999)

She was very upset because her mother brought cookies to the convent and the Mother Nun wouldn't give them to her and scolded her for wanting them. She explains in this story how they starved the women all the time. It's a sad story.

She ended up escaping and finding the true Jesus. However, she explains how many nuns died in that convent and never knew the real Jesus.

She also explained how they would kill babies that were born through the sexual abuse.

According to this woman, the perversion is atrocious. The image they provide to the world is opposite of the true image. This can be said for this whole apostasy. You can also watch her testimony on YouTube here - https://youtu.be/sVVYtwyCm9E

More Information About Ecumenical Movement

The whole purpose of the EM is to be more current, relevant, up-to-date, postmodern and relatable to the new generation. Well, this is totally against scripture. According to Dean Odle, "Walking in love is about keeping the commandments of God, knowing Him intimately, and being willing to speak all of the truths in the Bible whether they are popular or not." (Odle, The Polluted Church; From Rome to Kansas City, 2012)

As you will notice in Book #2 The American Idols, this is an idol when we put political correctness over scripture! Almost all 40 idols address apostasy!

Dean Odle speaks about the church partnering with Rome, "They just keep pouring the wine of their idolatry down the throats of the people of the world and the church and now many are drunk with it." (Odle, The Polluted Church; From Rome to Kansas City, 2012)

EM Attack on Evangelical Christians – The Right

Bride, I must put these random thoughts in this book when it comes to me because there is so much research I've conducted over the year and it must be noted. The reason President Trump joined with the evangelicals is because we are the only ones who would speak out against the Beast. Keep your enemies closer. So, President Trump's presidency has been in the planning since the 90s.

So, the propaganda is to demonize the President and his followers. However, it is all a stage. You will learn in this book that they have infiltrated both the left side (progressive – liberal people) and the right side (conservatives). They have reached us as the Bible says, "To all men be all people". In my views the NAR is the infiltration on the right and the EC is the infiltration on the left.

The left also includes the Black Liberation Theology. This is a root of Barack Obama and his spiritual mentor. This theology hates everything white and traditional Christianity. The way they are attacking us today we can see that this theology is one of the roots.

Ecumenical Movement vs. Pentecostals/Evangelicals

So, the Ecumenical Movement has this document where the president of the World Council of Churches addresses Rome about the problem they're having with Pentecostals. So, listen to how they describe us in the following documentation from the WCC meeting!

"Evangelical" is a more elastic term than "Pentecostal," and therefore discussion about the presence or absence of evangelicals in ecumenical arenas is more complex. More damaging is the public perception generally promoted by the media that at least in North America, the category of "evangelical" refers automatically to Christians whose social views and political muscle is synonymous with the Religious Right. Again, this is a stereotype that seriously misrepresents the realities on the ground and inhibits ecumenical engagement. (WCC, 2005)

We all know that the Pentecostals and Charismatics have always been the root and foundation of the right. We are the conservative voice because we believe the Bible literally.

Now, as time went on since this meeting, the groups began pulling the Bible away from Pentecostals and went more towards experience and feelings. Therefore, they have infiltrated with music. It's this "hippie spirit" I keep talking about. I will explain more later. Let's continue with this document from the worldwide headquarters dated in 2005.

Following World War II, a network of evangelical institutional structures emerged that were formed generally in reaction against emerging ecumenical bodies. Thus, in the U.S. the National Association of Evangelicals was formed as an alternative to the perceived 'liberalism' of the National Council of Churches.

That pattern became an unfortunate American religious "export" around the world. When the World Evangelical Fellowship was established, it provided a global fellowship to evangelical churches and bodies not willing to trust the opportunities and agenda offered by the World Council of Churches. (WCC, 2005)

Notice how that paragraph stated how America basically formed a watchdog group against this ecumenism and has blocked them! Too funny! Way to go America! Protect our country from this liberalist agenda!

Top Characters in Ecumenical Movement
Rick Warren, Saddleback Church

It's a known fact that Rick Warren, famous author of *Purpose Driven Life* (best seller book), is ecumenical to the bone. He is a puppet of the Pope for sure. He represents the left side of the church (evangelical). He is the liberal side. He is also famous for the phrase Chrislam (mixing of Christianity and Islam).

He is also the pastor who was the pastor at President Obama's inauguration. He has sold out for sure.

Through my research I have discovered that he is a main catalyst for the push in the United States. He is over thousands of churches due to this *Purpose Driven Life* book. I could write a whole book on this man. I will just write a few facts about his ecumenical history:

• According to author Roger Oakland in his book, *Faith Undone*, he is describing the rising of the Emergent Church and Rick Warren's participation, "While Leadership Network was the catalyst that initially launched the emerging church, many other ministries and organizations have helped to fuel it. One of the major catalysts is Rick Warren. Warren's support for Buford and Leadership Network goes back many years. Warren endorsed Buford's 1994 book, Halftime, calling Buford a 'rare individual'. But perhaps more important is the fact that Warren shared Buford's great admiration for Drucker. ...Warren's view that Buford was a 'rare individual' was mutual. ...Warren's role was also vital to the emerging church's growth." (Oakland, Faith Undone, 2007)

• Warren's push for unity among religions inspired him to pray in the name of Isa (the false Jesus of Islam) at President Obama's inauguration in 2008. His name can be found on a document called, "Loving God and Neighbor Together: A Christian Response to (the Muslim document) a Common Word Between Us and You", which plainly states that Muslims and Christians worship the same god. This is total blasphemy of the One True God

Jehovah and his son Jesus Christ because the God of Abraham and Allah are NOT the same being.

Warren has since tried to downplay his role in this apostasy, but he has not renounced his participation. (Odle, The Polluted Church; From Rome to Kansas City, 2012)

• On the World Council for Church's website, they have a document called The Future of Ecumenism in the 21st Century dated October 2005 in which Rick Warren is a participant. Can you believe that? This in 2005. Look at him today.

When you partner with this movement they will give you power, platforms, and elevate you. This document states, "Ecumenism in this, the 21st Century must find fresh forms of expression, new avenues to overcome divisions, and inspiring vision that spiritually engages the churches and its members in this calling." (WCC, 2005)

This is where Rick fits in the picture. In 2005 they are seeking this goal. Look what has happened to his life since then. Let's continue...

As a global strategist, Dr. Warren advises leaders in the public, private, and faith sectors on leadership development, poverty, health, education, and faith in culture. He has been invited to speak at the United Nations, the World Economic Forum in Davos, the African Union, the Council on Foreign Relations, Harvard's Kennedy School of Government, TIME's Global Health Summit, and numerous congresses around the world. TIME magazine named him one of "15 World Leaders Who Mattered Most in 2004" and in 2005 one of the "100 Most Influential People in the World." Also, in 2005 U.S. News & World Report named him one of "America's 25 Best Leaders." (Warren, 2020)

See how his website describes his success:

As a pastor, Rick founded Saddleback Church in Lake Forest, Calif., in 1980 with one family. Today, it is an evangelical congregation averaging 22,000 weekly attendees, a 120-acre campus, and has more than 300 community ministries to groups such as prisoners, CEOs, addicts, single parents, and those with HIV/AIDS.

He also leads the Purpose Driven Network of churches, a global coalition of congregations in 162 countries. More than 400,000 ministers and priests have been trained worldwide, and almost 157,000 church leaders subscribe to the Ministry ToolBox, his weekly newsletter. His previous book, The Purpose Driven Church is listed in "100 Christian Books That Changed the 20th Century." Forbes magazine called it "the best book on entrepreneurship, management, and leadership in print."

Kenneth Copeland – Believer's Voice of Victory

Now I'm moving on to Kenneth Copeland. I believe he is the representative for the right – the Faith Movement. He's known in some circles as the Father of Faith. He is the Pope's right-hand man for the Pentecostal people. He held a conference for his followers and the guest speaker was a representative for the Pope. This gentleman's name was Tony. They all three (Pope, Copeland & Tony) shared with the world that they were coming together in unity. They were dropping the differences.

The video is all over YouTube. I encourage you to watch it. Many people that have seen him since this encounter all agree that he does not even look the same. He looks like he's been taken over.

I'm not trying to be mean, I'm just stating that it's obvious. I will show you how he has partnered with the Pope and the apostasy:

• On Charisma Magazine, "James and Betty Robison, co- hosts of the Life Today television program, and Kenneth Copeland, co-host of Believer's Voice of Victory, met the Roman Pontiff at the Vatican on Tuesday. The meeting lasted almost three hours and included a private luncheon with Pope Francis.

Mr. Robison told the Fort Worth Star Telegram, 'This meeting was a miracle.... This is something God has done. God wants his arms around the world. And he wants Christians to put his arms around the world by working together.'" (Wiles, 2014)

In addition:

The ecumenical meeting in Rome was organized by Episcopal Bishop Tony Palmer. Rev. Palmer is an ordained bishop in the Communion of Evangelical Episcopal Churches, a break-away alliance of charismatic Anglican-Episcopal churches.

Bishop Palmer is also the Director of The Ark Community, an international interdenominational Convergent Church online community, and is a member of the Roman Catholic Ecumenical Delegation for Christian Unity and Reconciliation.

Bishop Palmer developed a friendship with Pope Francis when the future Roman Pontiff was a Catholic official in Argentina. Prior to becoming a CEEC bishop, Rev. Palmer was the director of the Kenneth Copeland Ministries' office in South Africa. He is married to an Italian Roman Catholic woman. He later moved to Italy and began working to reconcile Roman Catholics and Protestants. Kenneth Copeland Ministries was one of Mr. Palmer's first financial contributors over 10 years ago in support of his ecumenical work in Italy.

Earlier this year, Pope Francis called Bishop Palmer to invite him to his residence in Vatican City.

During the meeting, Bishop Palmer suggested that the Pope record a personal greeting on Mr. Palmer's iPhone to be delivered to Kenneth Copeland. Mr. Copeland showed the Papal video greeting to a conference of Protestant ministers who were meeting at Mr. Copeland's Eagle Mountain International Church near Fort Worth,

Texas. In the video, Pope Francis expressed his desire for Christian unity with Protestants. Later, James Robison telecasted the video on his daily TV program, Life Today. (Wiles, 2014)

That article pretty much explains it all. The latest news is that Copeland participated in an event called Kairos 2017. This was an ecumenical event where they were celebrating the 500th year of celebration for the Protestant Reformation. Here's what the website says about this event:

Kairos 2017 – Unity in Christ – So the World Will Know Him Celebrating A Year of Destiny

"I in them and You in Me – so that they may be brought to complete unity." John 17:23

Honoring the Significance of 2017 for the Church Internationally:

40 year anniversary of the Ecumenical Charismatic Conference in Kansas City (1977)

500 year anniversary of the Protestant Reformation (1517)

50 year anniversary of the Catholic Charismatic Renewal (1967)

50 year anniversary of the Messianic Movement (1967)

In October 2017, this will be an historic conference with leaders from Catholic, Protestant & Orthodox Churches. This year is a year of destiny.

We believe that GOD is calling His people to unity in Christ, as Jesus prayed in John 17. "...so the world would believe that GOD sent His Son." This unity is not about doctrines, but on spiritual unity, recognizing the contributions of each diverse group, the hope of which can bring healing and revival to the nation! Speakers are:

KEYNOTE: Cardinal Daniel DiNardo

Cardinal Daniel DiNardo is the archbishop of Galveston-Houston and pastor to its 1.3 million Catholics (& 4+ million non-Catholics). He requests each of us to deeply internalize the meaning of every human person. archgh.org

KEYNOTE: Kenneth Copeland

Kenneth Copeland is known worldwide as a speaker, author, television minister and recording artist. A household name, his ministry specializes in Biblical teaching that focuses on faith, love, healing, prosperity and restoration. kcm.org

Bride, you need to check out the speakers at this event.

These meeting was to declare that the reformation no longer exists. The Catholic church signed an agreement with the Protestants and it is now over.

The Truth About Kairos 2017

This event is celebrating a huge shift that happened in 2017. All the different things that have happened in 2017 alone.

As Kenneth Copeland is preaching at the event, he is trying to convince the attendees that this is all God-ordained to come together in unity. It is sad.

Check it out yourself Bride at www.kairos2017.com.

Ecumenical Denomination in the United States Formed Specifically for Ecumenism

There is a whole denomination in America that is nothing but ecumenical. This denomination focuses on blending everything and becoming inclusive. It is a lot like the Emergent Church, however Rome oversees this specific denomination. Check out The Evangelical Covenant Church.

Here is information from their website: (please notice on their site where they say but not – this means the other evangelical churches – ours – the traditional)

Welcome to the Evangelical Covenant Church

We are a multiethnic movement of 875 congregations in the United States and Canada with ministries on five continents of the world. The ECC values the Bible as the word of God, the gift of God's grace through faith in Jesus Christ, the call to extend God's love to a hurting world, and the strength that comes from unity within diversity.

The Evangelical Covenant Church is: Evangelical, but not exclusive Biblical, but not doctrinaire Traditional, but not rigid Congregational, but not independent Vision for Mission

We covenant: to cultivate communities of worship committed to: prayer, preaching, and study of the word; the celebration of the sacraments; and fellowship across gender, race, age, culture, and class.

To equip loving, giving, growing Christians to reach out with the good news of Jesus Christ – evangelizing the lost, ministering to those in need, and seeking justice for the oppressed.

Facts: We are committed to reach people with new life in Christ, and then to help them grow deeper in Christ. It is a lifelong journey of faith. (TECC, 2018)

These churches are also growing rapidly. You will notice when you sift through their website and most all the other websites that they avoid key words that set triggers like ecumenical. You can check out their website at covchurch.org. I'm making you aware so that you can see if any are in your city.

Final Notes About Ecumenical Strategy

If the church will really pay attention, the Roman Catholic Church, the Vatican, is waging war against the Protestants; they're just using the best tactic ever! They're ripping us from the inside out. They are after the conservative side (the ones that won't take the mark or become a part of their one world religion). They are attacking the old, white evangelical base. You will see it all through this book. I'm not meaning this mean against the black church but look at the demonic assault against white people today. Also, look at how most of the black church flipped. They went liberal to the core.

So, the Catholic church has decided to lie, twist our own words, deceive, doctrinal deception and bring confusion in to rip us apart. They've grabbed us on right & left.

Everything leads back to Rome. They want a Eucharistic Jesus (everyone doing communion their way). They are the snake and the Orthodox Jews implementing the Noahide Laws are the knife to the church.

Additional Notes About Bibles

Now they have an ecumenical bible by Cokesbury (bookstore for United Methodist:

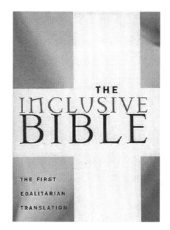

The Inclusive Bible
The First Egalitarian Translation

- By **Priests for Equality**

While this new Bible is certainly an inclusive-language translation, it is much more: it is a re-imagining of the scriptures and our relationship to them. Not merely replacing male pronouns, the translators have rethought what kind of language has built barriers between the text and its readers. Seeking to be faithful to the original languages, they have sought new and non-sexist ways to express the same ancient truths.

The Inclusive Bible is a fresh, dynamic translation into modern English, carefully crafted to let the power and poetry of the language shine forth--particularly when read aloud--giving it an immediacy and intimacy rarely found in traditional translations of the Bible. The Inclusive Bible contains both the Old and the New Testaments. (Cokesbury, 2020)

The Passion Translation is just as bad. Produced by NAR.

.

5

New Apostolic Reformation (NAR)

As stated earlier, there really is no way to pinpoint what this group believes because they do not have a certain rulebook. Since C. Peter Wagner died Chuck Pierce took his place. One of the head organizations is ICAL. (International Coalition of Apostolic Leaders).

However, although I believe Rick Joyner (one of their leaders) is a part of NAR, he provides insight into why this is that case, "Many movements that start to emphasize Kingdom theology open the door to a control spirit. We need to understand why." (Joyner, 2006). He continues to explain in this article that God wants a people that will honor him out of love and not as servants. This will mean that in his interpretation people who view themselves as servants to God are controlling. They are free if they operate out of love?

He explains that "This actually is a part of the initial reason God created mankind and gave us free will. He did not want robots, but a family and friends. He wanted cooperation based on love, not fear or compulsion." (Joyner, 2006). Notice the date written. (2006).

I heard a sermon with Bill Johnson preaching and he said basically the same thing that God wanted us as friends, not as servants. "You know the difference between a servant and a friend. Servants are task oriented. Their entire focus is on completing the list of assignments – the commands. Obedience is always important for the believer, but a friend just has a different motivation. A servant obtains his favor by what he does. A friend by the relationship. John 15 says that a servant doesn't know what the master is doing. A servant doesn't have access to the inner-workings, motivations, thoughts of the master. The implication is that the friend does. So as the servant's main goal is to do whatever is said. The friend's main goal is the heart of the friend; the thoughts, the impressions. That's not meeting a quota. It's bringing a joy through friendship." (Johnson, Don't Worship the Bible - Bill Johnson, 2014)

As I stated earlier in the book, we are servants of God. In the Book of Revelation, he talks about us as servants. Remember too that the Lord showed me that we are rewarded for being a servant. It's all in the obedience and our mission. There is nothing more important on this Earth than our obedience to God.

NAR has taken it to the extreme of friendship mixed with mysticism and occultism. They are boundaryless. They operate with no boundaries. If someone says they went to the courts of Heaven and fought their case standing next to the Devil no one challenges it.

It's an everything-goes type of religion. The sad thing is that they have mixed with Kundalini spirit, etc. I will explain more later.

Now, if you are to look at Christianity in the way that ministers like this describe, then we are all to be just friends of God. However, think about God with all of humanity in the word of God.

Did he ever act like just their friend or was he daddy God? If you consider the spirit of this group (EM, NAR & EC), then you will see that it is like a bunch of entitled spoiled people. It is prideful and haughty.

It is the same way with our children when we do not correct them and only befriend them.

Have you ever seen good parenting like that? Parents are always parents. They are always seen as the authoritative one. If you take away the correction and oversight, then you open yourself up to deception. I remember how my mom always kept her eye out for me. She was more of a parent than a friend.

When you love someone you correct them. You help them to see the truth. It takes energy to correct and discipline.

Not only is the spirit about NAR like a rebellious house because they do not have discipline through correction, etc., but they also do not have a structure with boundaries. They do not want restraints. Restraints = 10 Commandments. Therefore, they say, "when you have Jesus, we no longer have to do the law."

Let's examine what the Bible says about friend with God.

Bill Johnson mentions John 15. Yes, it does say that "If you keep my commandments you are a friend." However, this is Jesus talking to his personal disciples/apostles. Guess what? Friend is mentioned 99 times in the Bible and servant is mentioned 885 times! So, which do you think is more important to God? Also, look at what it says in the end of time in Revelation:

> *Revelation 22:3 And there shall be no more curse:*
> *but the throne of God and of the Lamb shall be in*
> *it; and his servants shall serve him:*
>
> *Revelation 22:6 And he said unto me, These sayings*
> *are faithful and true: and the Lord God of the holy*
> *prophets sent his angel to shew unto his servants*
> *the things which must shortly be done.*

What is this saying? This is saying that when we are in the new city THAT WE WILL STILL BE SERVANTS TO GOD! So, in the beginning of time and the end of time we're still servants! Also, look at Jesus' whole life! Was he a servant or a master?

Was he dominant over us? NO! He was a servant and taught us how to serve. He taught us how to go low. The whole point of Christianity is to be humbled and prefer others above ourselves, etc. If we're elevated to a friend, then how can we be humbled? When I think of a friend, I think of equal status. Look at this scripture:

> *Romans 9:20 Nay but, O man, who art thou that*
> *repliest against God? Shall the thing formed say to*
> *him that formed it, Why hast thou made me thus?*

This is basically saying, "Who are you to tell God what to do?" I still refer to the Dominionism theology that the NAR believes where they are superpowers and have dominion over everything. I understand that we mature to the level that we know God's heart on most things, but not all things. We're not that privileged. We have limited knowledge. This is the difference between a servant and a friend. A Servant of a king honors and respects his king.

It reverences the position he plays in the relationship and causes us to desire to serve and please the king. If I'm a king's friend, then I may not have as much reverence for him because now we're on equal ground.

I will feel bolder in my approach to him because of my status. I may be more willing to express my opposition to his thinking because we're on equal ground. As a servant, I do not question his rulings because the king knows best. I may ask why, but not demand as the Dominionism thinking may allude to.

Servant = respect and honor/ Friend = more laid back and even What about when we die. The Bible says that when stand before the throne, we hope to hear, "Well done, thy good and faithful servant."

> *Matthew 25:21 His lord said unto him, Well done, thou good and faithful servant: thou hast been faithful over a few things, I will make thee ruler over many things: enter thou into the joy of thy lord.*

It does not say, "Welcome to Heaven you friend!" God could also say, "You call me Lord Lord but I know you not!"

> *Matthew 7:21-23 21 Not everyone that saith unto me, Lord, Lord, shall enter into the kingdom of heaven; but he that doeth the will of my Father which is in heaven. 22 Many will say to me in that day, Lord, Lord, have we not prophesied in thy name? and in thy name have cast out devils? and in thy name done many wonderful works? 23 And then will I profess unto them, I never knew you: depart from me, ye that work iniquity.*

It all boils down to knowing sin and its place in your life. Allowing God to correct you and change you. If you don't allow God to transform you and be willing to conform into the image of Christ, then you're not a Christian. Christianity is constantly being delivered and set free. It's allowing God to renew our minds.

This group is designed to REFORM the way Christianity is enacted today. This is a rebellious house because they are rebelling against God's design.

They Want to Redesign the
Structure of Churches/Kingdom

The New Apostolic Reformation (NAR) crowd wants to cancel out the old way of doing church through a regular church building, a pastor, and the way that our current system does it now. They want to bring in the five-fold ministry gifts into a whole new setup. They feel like we are doing it wrong and leaving out the positions of the apostle and prophet. Really, they are taking us back into elitism and hierarchy like the Catholic Church. The Bible says we are all equal. There is no Jew, Greek, Gentile etc., in the Kingdom. We are all equal! Those positions – apostle, prophet, pastor, teacher, etc., are positions that any of us can fill at any time. Some people try to elevate themselves and say, "I operate in all 5". Yes. Any of us can.

Let's Examine the Apostleship in the New Testament

(This of course will all be past the Book of Acts)

> **1 Corinthians 12:27-29 27 Now ye are the body of Christ, and members in particular. 28 And God hath set some in the church, first apostles,**

secondarily prophets, thirdly teachers, after that miracles, then gifts of healings, helps, governments, diversities of tongues. 29 Are all apostles? are all prophets? are all teachers? are all workers of miracles?

2 Corinthians 11:12-14 12 But what I do, that I will do, that I may cut off occasion from them which desire occasion; that wherein they glory, they may be found even as we. 13 For such are false apostles, deceitful workers, transforming themselves into the apostles of Christ. 14 And no marvel; for Satan himself is transformed into an angel of light.

2 Corinthians 12:12 Truly the signs of an apostle were wrought among you in all patience, in signs, and wonders, and mighty deeds.

Revelation 2:1-3 1 Unto the angel of the church of Ephesus write; These things saith he that holdeth the seven stars in his right hand, who walketh in the midst of the seven golden candlesticks; 2 I know thy works, and thy labour, and thy patience, and how thou canst not bear them which are evil: and thou hast tried them which say they are apostles, and are not, and hast found them liars: 3 And hast borne, and hast patience, and for my name's sake hast laboured, and hast not fainted.

As you notice, the word apostle is not mentioned very much in the Bible.

Yes, it says we do have the five-fold, but do you see anywhere in the Bible that God says, "In the last days the five-fold offices will be restored, and a new kingdom will reign on the Earth of apostles as the head of the church now. This group will overthrow the whole current system and I will have all the glory in this revolution (reformation)".

NO. It is because it is NOT BIBLICAL. Bride, I encourage you to try to search it on the web yourself as to how this New Apostolic Reformation believes. It does not even have a head or any type of document leading it. Why? Because it's a spirit controlling it. It causes all the people that attach to it to begin to prophecy and speak words over it to convince the masses that this is okay. However, how can it be okay when it's not scriptural?

The Bible mentions the word apostle one (1) time in the Book of Revelation when it's not talking specifically about Jesus' disciples. Which time you ask? It's the time when Jesus is talking about one of the seven churches not being right with him.

He says the apostles who are spewing lies. Guess what it does say a lot in the Book of Revelation? Prophets! Yes!! In the whole Bible the word apostle is mentioned 80 times. The word prophet is mentioned 454 times! Can you believe it? WOW! You tell me which one is more important. Why is the prophet more important? Because it is the office warning people and keeping them on track. The apostle is the administrative side. The prophet is the voice of God side.

Notice that there are women as prophets!

Exodus 15:20 And Miriam the prophetess, the sister of Aaron, took a timbrel in her hand; and all the women went out after her with timbrels and with dances.

Judges 4:4 And Deborah, a prophetess, the wife of Lapidoth, she judged Israel at that time.

Luke 2:36 And there was one Anna, a prophetess, the daughter of Phanuel, of the tribe of Aser: she was of a great age, and had lived with an husband seven years from her virginity;

False Prophets & Apostles in Bible

Deuteronomy 13:5 And that prophet, or that dreamer of dreams, shall be put to death; because he hath spoken to turn you away from the Lord your God, which brought you out of the land of Egypt, and redeemed you out of the house of bondage, to thrust thee out of the way which the Lord thy God commanded thee to walk in. So shalt thou put the evil away from the midst of thee.

Deuteronomy 18:20 But the prophet, which shall presume to speak a word in my name, which I have not commanded him to speak, or that shall speak in the name of other gods, even that prophet shall die.

Deuteronomy 18:22 When a prophet speaketh in the name of the Lord, if the thing follow not, nor come to pass, that is the thing which the Lord hath not spoken, but the prophet hath spoken it presumptuously: thou shalt not be afraid of him.

1 Kings 13:26 And when the prophet that brought him back from the way heard thereof, he said, It is the man of God, who was disobedient unto the word of the Lord: therefore the Lord hath delivered him unto the lion, which hath torn him, and slain him, according to the word of the Lord, which he spake unto him.

1 Kings 19:14 And he said, I have been very jealous for the Lord God of hosts: because the children of Israel have forsaken thy covenant, thrown down thine altars, and slain thy prophets with the sword; and I, even I only, am left; and they seek my life, to take it away.

Zechariah 13:1-3 - 1 In that day there shall be a fountain opened to the house of David and to the inhabitants of Jerusalem for sin and for uncleanness. 2 And it shall come to pass in that day, saith the Lord of hosts, that I will cut off the names of the idols out of the land, and they shall no more be remembered: and also I will cause the prophets and the unclean spirit to pass out of the land.

3 And it shall come to pass, that when any shall yet prophesy, then his father and his mother that begat him shall say unto him, Thou shalt not live; for thou speakest lies in the name of the Lord: and his father and his mother that begat him shall thrust him through when he prophesieth.

Matthew 24:11 And many false prophets shall rise, and shall deceive many.

Matthew 24:24 For there shall arise false Christs, and false prophets, and shall shew great signs and wonders; insomuch that, if it were possible, they shall deceive the very elect.

Luke 6:26 Woe unto you, when all men shall speak well of you! for so did their fathers to the false prophets.

Acts 7:52 Which of the prophets have not your fathers persecuted? and they have slain them which shewed before of the coming of the Just One; of whom ye have been now the betrayers and murderers:

Acts 13:6 And when they had gone through the isle unto Paphos, they found a certain sorcerer, a false prophet, a Jew, whose name was Barjesus:

James 5:9-11 9 Grudge not one against another, brethren, lest ye be condemned: behold, the judge standeth before the door.

10 Take, my brethren, the prophets, who have spoken in the name of the Lord, for an example of suffering affliction, and of patience. 11 Behold, we count them happy which endure. Ye have heard of the patience of Job, and have seen the end of the Lord; that the Lord is very pitiful, and of tender mercy.

2 Peter 2:1-3 1 But there were false prophets also among the people, even as there shall be false teachers among you, who privily shall bring in damnable heresies, even denying the Lord that bought them, and bring upon themselves swift destruction.

2 And many shall follow their pernicious ways; by reason of whom the way of truth shall be evil spoken of. 3 And through covetousness shall they with feigned words make merchandise of you: whose judgment now of a long time lingereth not, and their damnation slumbereth not.

1 John 4:1 Beloved, believe not every spirit, but try the spirits whether they are of God: because many false prophets are gone out into the world.

Revelation 2:20 Notwithstanding I have a few things against thee, because thou sufferest that woman Jezebel, which calleth herself a prophetess, to teach and to seduce my servants to commit fornication, and to eat things sacrificed unto idols.

> **Revelation 18:24 And in her was found the blood of prophets, and of saints, and of all that were slain upon the Earth.**

Bride, notice how many times it mentions false prophets. There is much more in the bible about it. It talks about how they will deceive us in the last days. It even talks about how the Antichrist will kill the prophets in the end.

It also talks about how if you call yourself a prophet and you're well-liked, then you are considered a false prophet. How can we say this? We can say this because as the scriptures above states, those that are true servants of God will be persecuted as Jesus was persecuted. If you're not being persecuted, then you're not doing something right. The devil can't stand truth.

When I studied 2 Chronicles, we studied about kings and God's heart towards sin. You learn in the old testament that false prophets are a judgment to the church. We want swelling prophecies so we shall get it! It's really sad when you think about it.

Leviathan, Jezebel & Cain Spirit

They all work together. Leviathan is the chief demon of pride. In the NAR movement they operate out of pride. This is why they think they can go to the courts of heaven and battle their own sins with Satan and God. They can tell the atmosphere what to do. They know it all. It's the ultimate form of pride. This is the Dominionism. This is also how they can partner with President Trump and excuse all of his prideful attitudes. This is judgment to the church because God is allowing us to see our own vomit. His prideful words, put-downs of other people and out-right nastiness in words is a reflection of the people he has partnered with.

This is also why he can partner with the LGBTQ and not hear how damning that is with God. Those same evangelicals party with the LGBTQ groups and invite them to their planning parties, etc. If they are so powerful, then why not speak to the Coronavirus and tell it to stop, etc.? Where do you draw the line?

At the last planning meeting they had for his #Trump2020 campaign, they had transgender guys performing for them and hosting a pool party, etc.

I even shared a picture on my Facebook wall of Donald Trump Jr and his girlfriend with the transgender singer, Ricky Rebel, with his penis bulge showing through his pants. It was gross. The comments were shock and awe over this picture. However, this isn't the half of what his family, evangelicals and his 2020 staff have partnered with. This is a sign of the power of Leviathan in all of this.

Right after I moved out of Washington DC, President Trump announced that Paula White had moved in. I do not believe this was a coincidence. She is the epitome of the apostasy. I could write a whole book about her rotten fruit. There are videos out there of her bragging about her and her husband's love of porn. Then she talks about sexual encounters with him before they're even married, etc. Much less how she stole sheep from other ministries (I know this first hand) and how she stole actual ministries. The proof is out there. Anyways, she moves in the White House and started a prayer initiative called **As One**. This is demonic to the core.

It is demonic because it's a deception. What they're not telling the evangelical church is how they have partnered with the LGBTQ and other faiths. This is what they mean by AS ONE.

The AS ONE movement actually started years ago with the same leaders who are now partnered with the POPE and have mixed Catholicism in with their meetings, etc. (Dutch Sheets, Cindy Jacobs, Lou Engle, etc.) This is the same group who does most of their conferences, book endorsements, etc. together.

They are in a stream of the church called the GLORY STREAM. The glory stream is a branch of Christianity that is focused on the extreme supernatural and their leaders are Dutch Sheets, Chuck Pierce, Lou Engle, and basically all those on President Trump's evangelical board.

This stream is the NAR. They are wanting to do away with the old order of church and bring in a new order.

It is odd to me that Kanye sings in one of his new songs about Jezebel doesn't bother him when I know that Jezebel is the one who holds him. Jezebel partners with the spirit of Antichrist. As far as the Cain Spirit – this spirit will be our very own brothers and sisters (supposed to be anyway) who will kill us in the future. They will be the Jesus freaks of the wrong Jesus kind who will call us judgmental and fundamentalist one day. They will kill us and feel like we are the betrayers of the universal Jesus movement. Remember Cain got jealous.

According to one of the leaders in Washington DC, the main merge of the leaders happened like this, "As Dutch, Lou Engle and Mike Bickle downloaded insight related to their respective ministries, it became clear that the Lord was orchestrating a Holy Spirit convergence. Mike Bickle, Lou Engle, and Dutch Sheets decided to enter into a covenantal relationship to join 3 streams of prayer they represented

Bridal intimacy, Nazarite passion, and Governmental authority in intercession into one mighty river. Again, this marriage of movements took place on the 20th anniversary of the IHOP movement, and it was this very night when Steve Shultz released my Call KC Wedding Word." (Hamill J. , 2002)

What is this New Order?

The new order is the one that is ecumenical. This new order breaks out of tradition, out of the four walls and now into houses, barns, and basically anything away from the traditional church. We all get it that the church has issues and problems, but this order wants to be a whole new reformation. I must say that they are pretty successful.

They (through media) now have their claws in almost all streams. They have infected every other stream.

This new order wants everything led by apostles and they want you to tithe unto them as they are your leader. They want all the catalysts in each city. They want the people who are talented and gifted so they can give them a title. A great example of this is one of their leaders, Jennifer, said that Kanye West is a prophet. See how they do? If you think Kanye West is a prophet then you are reading another Bible. A prophet will require everything. Kanye refuses to give up his money and power…so no, he's not a prophet. However, this is a great example of how they want control of every powerful person. They have the president of the United States. Or does he have them? They're all working together.

So, the new order is pulling the church away from the fundamental doctrines of the past.

They are going away from doctrine and into mystical music, mystical teaching and practices.

Dominionism

NAR believed that we are to have dominion over the Earth in every way. Yes, I told you earlier that I believe we have dominion to a certain extent.

For instance, if a tornado is coming, then how do you know it's God's will to stop it? What if it is judgment? Who are we to make that call? Do we think we have enough dominion to overpower God? See the difference? Now, we can pray for God to protect OUR HOUSE AND BELONGINGS. Why? Because he shows us in his word that he is our protector and guard. He is a shield about us.

According to this apologist who studies NAR, this is her assessment; "Dominionism is the erroneous belief that Christians have a mandate to build the 'kingdom of God' on Earth, restoring paradise, by progressively and supernaturally transforming themselves and others as well as all societal institutions through subduing and ruling the Earth by whatever means possible, including using technology, science and psycho-social engineering; and then and only then will a 'Christ' manifest his presence on Earth." (Erdmann, 2013)

Now that I've researched for six months, I am more convinced than ever that when the leaders say "Christ", most of them do not mean the one that we know. They believe in Christ-Consciousness or universe. They have blended so much with the other religions.

How NAR Views Eschatology (End of the World)

This is very challenging to pinpoint because they do not have a written one-believe-all statement.

So, I will show you what their leaders believe, and you can take it from there.

Joseph Mattera is the head of the International Coalition of Prophets (ICOP), which is partnered with the ICAL (International Coalition of Apostolic Leaders). This is one aspect of his eschatology, "Others, like myself, have a view like amillennialists that the reign of Christ is not literally a physical 1,000 year future period. I believe this because Scripture teaches the church (in heaven and on Earth) already began to reign with Christ since the inauguration of the kingdom (Mark 1:15, Romans 5:17, and Ephesians 1:17-2:26). Post-millennialists allow for both a spiritual reign in heaven and a gradual manifestation of Christ's kingdom on the Earth before His return since they believe the biblical covenants (starting with Genesis 1:28) are still in force on the Earth and revealed by the blessings and curses God bestows on individuals and nations commensurate to the degree they accept or reject the laws of God and the Gospel of Christ." (Mattera, 2017)

According to this article, you can't help but to decipher that he does not believe in a rapture, or a second-coming of Jesus, or a 1,000 year Millennial Reign. Now, from my research I'm discovering that most NAR people believe that Jesus fulfilled everything in 70AD.

Therefore, they are working so hard now to create a literal kingdom on the Earth. Many of their critics accuse them of believing they're little gods and have authority over everything, to include the seven mountains of culture. They believe they must takeover the whole Earth to prepare it for Jesus return. They do not agree that an antichrist is coming, mark of the beast, end of times as we know it.

Most of them do not even believe in sin. It is so diluted and polluted.

I have heard some of them preach that the Tree of Knowledge of Good and Evil does not even exist anymore when you get saved. Jesus died once and for all and sin no longer touches you.

IHOP's Contemplative Prayer & New Age

Contemplative prayer is one of the gateways of the deception. When people open their minds and souls to visualizations, bridal paradigm, going into the third heaven when they should not be there, (they call this "abandonment"), then we open it up to the Kundalini spirit (false spirit).

One of the main teachers today of this false prayer strategy is Mike Bickle (pastor of *International House of Prayer* in Kansas City). I read his document that he teaches in his school and this is a little section of it:

Anyway, I like the whole Barnes & Noble deal. I've been going there for ten or fifteen years. First there was a book on prayer here and there, then they got this big religious section, and then there were one or two books on contemplation. They call them mystics. I don't use the word mystics, even though it's a legitimate term. I don't want to fight that war. There were so many people who use the word mystics who were so off. I don't want to argue for them. I don't want to say who was and who wasn't, so I'm just saying, 'contemplative prayer', but I mean the mystics. (Bickle, 2001)

Notice how he used the term "mystics". According to the dictionary, mystics is defined as "mystical, which means comes from eastern origin. Mysticism, the practice of religious ecstasies (religious experiences during alternate states of consciousness), together with whatever ideologies, ethics, rites, myths, legends, and magic may be related to them." (Britannica, 2018)

Look at further information in this article! Pretty shocking!

The term mystic is derived from the Greek noun mystes, which originally designated an initiate of a secret cult or mystery religion.

In Classical Greece (5th–4th century BCE) and during the Hellenistic Age (323 BCE–330 CE), the rites of the mystery religions were largely or wholly secret. The term mystes is itself derived from the verb myein ("to close," especially the eyes or mouth) and signified a person who kept a secret. Early Christianity appropriated the technical vocabulary of the Hellenistic mysteries but later disavowed secrecy, resulting in a transformation of the meaning of mystes. In subsequent Christian usage, mystes, or mystic, referred to practitioners of doctrinally acceptable forms of religious ecstasy. (Britannica, 2018)

This form of prayer opens the door. Listen to what author Dean Odle says, "The trojan horse that has been accepted within every part of the church is a deception called 'contemplative prayer'. Some call it meditation, soaking or centering prayer." (Odle, The Polluted Church; From Rome to Kansas City, 2012) He goes on to say that it is full of occult techniques taught by eastern mysticism, etc. He also mentions visiting the 3rd heaven at will (same as courts of heaven).

He also describes this as, "This New Age style of 'praying', as well as other pagan practices has crept into once solid evangelical and charismatic churches. These practices have been accepted by some of the most well-known Christian leaders and they are opening themselves and their followers up to demon spirits and great deception through the repackaged meditative practices of eastern religions." (Odle, The Polluted Church; From Rome to Kansas City, 2012)

He further explains how he has seen others fade of into universalism and other occult teachings. I agree with this thinking because in my research I've noticed how it taints Christians like a frog in cold water and boils to death slowly. It deceives them.

Mike Bickle's OneThing Conference

Although he has officially ended this in 2019, it must be examined. Once a year IHOP sponsor's a yearly conference at the end of the year after Christmas. This conference is famous in the Charismatic world. In 2019 it was their last year. However, we still must examine this. Through my research I discovered that they have a Catholic one as well at the same time or right after. It's called the *Catholic Track*. Now, what they do is they have a mix of speakers at both events. So, basically, he's went totally ecumenical.

This is a very sad thing because I believe probably 90% of what he teaches except for his methods of prayer. Not only has his awesome worship team taught the Catholics on their techniques and ways, but they open their church's doors to the Catholics for events in their building (thus the OneThing, Kairos, etc.)

NAR Focuses on the Experience versus the Word

Like I said earlier in the book, this is not discounting genuine miracles. God can do anything he wants all by himself. I'm talking about the spirit of this movement. They heavily focus on the "glory realm, supernatural, gold dust, gems, etc." I'm merely stating that we cannot trust in these things as a measurement of what a Christian is or a ministry.

We must agree with the word of God in our teachings and actions in ministry. Can we back it up with the word of God?

Many religions heal people. Even the Chinese have theirs, "Qigong is a Chinese word that simply means energy work. It is an ancient holistic healing system and alternative medicine that has been used in the Far East for centuries to help with many serious health conditions. In China Qigong is used to:

- Relieve Pain and Stress
- Increase Energy & Stamina
- Alleviate Anxiety and Depression
- Overcome Insomnia
- Boost the Immune System
- Balance the Emotions
- Calm and Relax the Mind & Body
- Enhance Creativity & Productivity
- Help Heal a Variety of Health Conditions by Balancing the Energy System

Traditional Chinese Medicine teaches when the energy in the body is flowing properly then good health and well-being is the result." (Mohoric, 2012)

New Age, Hindu and other religions do supernatural things. In the end this will be used against us because the one world religion will be doing this with the Antichrist and we can't fall for it. Look at these scriptures:

> *2   John 1:7 - For many deceivers are entered into the world, who confess not that Jesus Christ is come in the flesh. This is a deceiver and an antichrist.*

2 Thessalonians 2:3-12 - Let no man deceive you by any means: for [that day shall not come], except there come a falling away first, and that man of sin be revealed, the son of perdition;

Revelation 19:20 - And the beast was taken, and with him the false prophet that wrought miracles before him, with which he deceived them that had received the mark of the beast, and them that worshipped his image. These both were cast alive into a lake of fire burning with brimstone.

Mark 13:6 - For many shall come in my name, saying, I am [Christ]; and shall deceive many.

This NAR Group Uses False Prophesy

In the Bible it talks about when false prophets speak only positive words and tell people it's going to be okay when it is not. They will answer to God about it. When they do not warn God's people about what's coming, this is grievous to God. You can almost spot a NAR prophecy a mile off. They all sound the same.

Not only that, but they are going to New Age Festivals, Gay Parades, going in bars, and acting like the world as "spiritual readers" etc. They are blending with the world to pray for healing and give "words" to sinners. The only words they need is repent!

I'm just going to give a few examples of a few ministries that are doing heretical things in the name of the prophetic:

• **Doug Addison** posts on his website how he's the forerunner of a new prophetic style. He's now prophesying to people's tattoos & piercings! He states that over one billion people on the planet have tattoos and piercings. This is on his website, "Take your prophetic ministry to the next level—discover how you can give powerful prophetic words to people through their tattoos and piercings." He also states, "Quite often There are hidden prophetic messages behind tattoo and piercings!

Since there are over a billion people that have tattoos or piercings, it opens an incredible way to start conversations and help people find the hidden prophetic messages behind the tattoos and the piercings they have. In this course you will discover:

o   Why people get tattoos
o   Tattoos in the Bible
o   Common tattoo designs and their meanings
o   How to recognize symbolic messages in tattoos
o   The significance of tattoo and piercing placement
o   How negative designs can have positive meanings
o   How to develop metaphoric thinking

• All of this comes from Doug Addison's many years of doing street ministry and seeing hundreds of lives changed through giving powerful prophetic words. Each lesson you'll learn comes from countless hours of street ministry. This will change the way you see people with tattoos and piercings. (Addison, 2018)

• **NAOITH College – Byron Bay** – (one of the endorsements of **Bill Johnson's Bethel Church**) – This is describing a class by leader Maria Mason, "We will look at the way four different Mystics, Thomas, Augustine, St Francis and Ignatius, approached their communion with God. We will see how our differing sacred

132

pathways reveal a greater way for connecting to God in our lives as we understand our own particular temperaments and unique ways of connecting to God" (NAIOTH COLLEGE, 2017)

• **Maria's husband, Phil Mason's website** explains why they take the soft compromising route when they go into these New Age festivals and do the same thing New Ager's do by prophesying and healing, "We only tell people what they need to know to prime them for a God encounter. We proclaim the Kingdom of Heaven and then we proceed to lay hands on people to bring them into an intense experience of the love and power of Christ. If they have a God encounter, as so many of the people who we minister to do, we take it a step further and tell them who it was who just healed or touched them; the love and power of Christ." (Mason, 2016)

• **Phil Mason** also explains how the traditional church has been in error, "Almost without exception most evangelicals throughout the centuries since the Reformation have proposed a one-dimensional solution to a two-dimensional problem of the human heart. Often, the glorious prophetic ministry of healing broken hearts, exemplified in the historical ministry of Jesus has been completely missing from the church's ministry repertoire. For many years I have been tracking on a specific spiritual journey. It has been a theological and experiential journey that has been shaped and molded by years of practical ministry experience to broken human lives. I am the pastor of a local church that cares for broken people. Along this journey I have stumbled upon a depth of revelation into certain aspects of the ministry of Jesus that desperately needs to be recovered by the wider church. In my personal quest to fully recover the "lost ministry of Jesus to the human heart" God has gradually imparted a deepening understanding into certain dimensions of ministry that have been completely overlooked by many historical and contemporary streams within the church." (Mason, The Glory of Christ's Kingdom, 2016)

The Bible says in 2 Chronicles 22-26 that it is a judgment to us when we have false prophets lying prophecies to us. It is a judgment to have our ears tickled. God sends a lying devil. It is so sad!

In 2 Chronicles 18 you will see that God sent a lying spirit into the false prophets **as a judgment against them**!

> *19 And the Lord said, Who shall entice Ahab king of Israel, that he may go up and fall at Ramothgilead? And one spake saying after this manner, and another saying after that manner.*
>
> *20 Then there came out a spirit, and stood before the Lord, and said, I will entice him. And the Lord said unto him, Wherewith?*
>
> *21 And he said, I will go out, and be a lying spirit in the mouth of all his prophets. And the Lord said, Thou shalt entice him, and thou shalt also prevail: go out, and do even so.*
>
> *22 Now therefore, behold, the Lord hath put a lying spirit in the mouth of these thy prophets, and the Lord hath spoken evil against thee.*

People believe all these false prophets because they're all speaking the same language. But how you say? Because they are deceived. Most of these NAR people are speaking "swelling words" to build up the human and not causing them to repent. What good are those swelling words going to do when the bottom falls out?

What good will it do when their day of martyrdom comes? The mark of the beast approaches them and then what? This is part of our judgment.

The very NAR people are the ones who went crazy on the prosperity gospel (give me $4,000 or $10,000 and I'll give you a word, or anoint you, etc). They went crazy with money and power. They are the very ones around the President now. They are the very ones partnering with other religions around the world, the Pope, Muslims, Hindus, Jews, etc. They are the very ones selling us out!

Selling us out to the highest bidder. Their greed has come to the surface. It is being exposed. God is separating the wheat from the chaff. The truth from false. There will be a war of the true and false prophets in the near future!

Berean Research Magazine: Leaders:

The founder of the New Apostolic Reformation is church growth specialist **C. Peter Wagner**. Wagner served as Professor of Church Growth at the Fuller Theological Seminary's School of World Missions until his retirement. Until recently he was president of *Global Harvest Ministries* and is currently Chancellor emeritus of the Wagner Leadership Institute. Prominent member of the *International Council of Apostles* - **Chuck Pierce** was his successor.

"Wagner, Chuck Pierce, Bob Jones, Paul Cain, Cindy Jacobs, Mike Bickle, Rick Joyner, Bill Johnson, Todd Bentley, Lou Engle, Becky Fischer. What the Bible says: 'But there were false prophets also among the people, even as there shall be false teachers among you, who privily shall bring in damnable heresies, even denying the Lord that bought them, and bring upon themselves swift destruction.' 2 Peter 2:1" (Spreeman, 2019)

So, Bride, when you see the characters above, check out who is associated to them and see what they're teaching. Make sure they're not making merchandise of you. Check out their main websites at ICAL.com, generals.org, etc. See who is associated to the above.

Also, these are the very ones partnering with the apostate Kanye West! Notice how quickly they give him a platform and endorsed him. They are pushing this man to the front who has not even repented or turned from calling himself God! He has not renounced his blasphemy. The elephant in the room has not been dealt with!

I wanted to point that out because not only is this New Jesus being pushed in the church, but it is in the music industry, politics, entertainment, and everywhere you look. The hippie days are back.

Bride, I encourage you to research these terms:
- Golden Age
- Aquarius Age
- Maitreya
- Meditation and the Master Within
- The New Age Peace Plan
- A Course in Miracles by Marianne Williamson
- Oprah and the New Age

The Fruit of the NAR

Let's examine their fruit for a moment. Let's look at **Todd Bentley**. All of their leadership to include **Rick Joyner** all backed him when he cheated on his wife and married his secretary or assistant. They publicly endorsed him and told everyone they are taking him under their wing. They are publicly endorsing a man who openly acts out in a spirit of kundalini.

His violent head shakes is a sure sign this is that false spirit. This glory stream backed him up and because of Bentley, we have a huge influx of tattoos in the church. As Dr. Phillip Morris stated from Houston Texas, "Leviathan is the chief demon of pride and when a person gets a tattoo they just invited that demon in." (See video at https://www.youtube.com/watch?v=eZYl1qwkNoU).

This is why a person who receives a tattoo is not satisfied and wants more. They also want to show off their tattoo(s) all the time. I have seen ministers (revivalists) who do this. They will be online preaching and salivating over their tattoos. They will be staring at them LIVE. Why do they wear clothing to show off their tattoos?

When Todd Bentley turned around and acted out in perversion again, they still backed him up and even to the third time where now the accusations are swinging, pedophilia, and all kinds of other deviancy. These leaders will not sit him down and require him to go through healing, etc.

Why? Because they are all so prideful and will continue ministry without rebuke. Did you know that the Bible says that God loves those that he rebukes? Yes. This is a part of Christianity. However, NAR people do not believe in that. They know it all.

Kanye West Shenanigans

The next situation to examine is the Kanye phenomenon. Why would the leaders (Evangelicals) partner with him?

Like I said about Jennifer (NAR) who proclaimed him as a prophet right off the bat. He still claims to be Yeezus and sells all his blasphemous clothing line, etc., but yet he is a prophet. Also, notice how this leadership network all wrote press releases within a week endorsing Kanye at the same time? This is not a coincidence. Then to have the mainstream media aboard and having him on all their channels in which they constantly trash President Trump? I don't buy it. To me, this is a real look into the apostasy because they are AS ONE.

These very same leaders are opening up their platforms for him to influence and taint millions of people. More about this later.

UN & LGBTQ Fruit of NAR

Another fruit is when I was at the UN in September 2019 with President Trump, I filmed the President's speech inside the United Nations building. I witnessed the evangelical leaders sitting on the front row with all other religions at the International Religious Freedom meeting. I was sick to my stomach witnessing them partner with the interfaith movement. It's a stench in God's nostrils. I was standing next to another Christian news outlet and we were all appalled at the obvious attachment to the unholy.

The church doesn't even know they partnered together because they have sugar-coated it as a good thing to fight for religious freedom.

However, let me tell you Bride, this organization in the State Department is the **front for the ecumenical movement**. It is a farce. It is pulling all religions together in the name of religious freedom but guess who is at the top of the food chain as far as who gets taken care of first? MUSLIMS! Yes, a very trustworthy informant told me this when I was in DC. I found this to be accurate when I worked the Ministerial Conference at the State Department and they only set up a tent for the Muslims to pray in! I asked them (because I was on the prayer team) why they didn't have one for Christians.

They said that anyone can pray in here if they want to. How crazy is that? What Christian would want to pray to our God when they are praying to their false god in the same room?

However, the point is that the NAR leadership has partnered with this group and trying to convince the evangelicals that it's good fruit. It's not. It's rotten. To top it off, I was in the meeting where all the nations were reporting back to the State Department about the advancements in religious freedom and guess what? They were reporting back as their push for LGBTQ in their nation! They often mentioned this because of Agenda 2030. Yes…LGBTQ is included in this mix! I wrote an article on WATB.tv about LGBTQ trying to become a religion. So, why doesn't our evangelical leaders tell us that they are in this group partnering with all this vomit? Because they want you to think it's all Pentecostal people and it is not. So, this fruit is rotten.

It is very suspicious to me their NAR leader, who is now in the White House, also partner with the *#WALKaway* LGBTQ group.

This group is the known LGBTQ people who are now traveling the country with donations from conservatives and Republicans to push their LGBTQ lifestyle in hopes to pull their kind over to Republicans. They also came to the *American Priority* conference and performed, etc. How can the evangelicals go to their parties and partner with this mess? Some people say that Trump is only doing this to get votes. It is sad that they will accept this as an excuse. Did he have to do it the first time? Why does he need them now? Why? Because now he knows he has us so he's going after the gays and colors. He WANTS THEM ALL.

I wrote the board and asked them for an interview, in which they turned it down. I also wrote back asking them for a written response as to why they are partnering with the LGBTQ.

They refused.. I was working in the White House as a reporter for a Christian news outlet and was wanting to know why our evangelicals are partnering with this mess. Shouldn't they answer to us? Are they not supposed to be our leaders? Do the evangelicals even care anymore? They have all blended together with the ungodly and this is their rotten fruit.

The Jesus Movement Again

This same group is pushing a new movement called the New Jesus Movement. They have now included Kanye in this mix. They are pushing **Lonnie Frisbee's** story as to why anyone can preach whether you are battling homosexuality like he did or whatever sin you're still in. It's an *anything goes* movement – inclusive. This is what **Lou Engle** says about it on a post on Facebook.

He is saying now that LOVE OVERLOOKS HOMOSEXUALITY AND PEOPLE'S "BEHAVIORS". He's comparing this revival coming (fake) to Lonnie Frisbee!

He was a homosexual on Saturday nights and preach on Sunday morning. He was one of the founders of Vineyard church (where Bill Johnson & IHOP began). Now they have made a movie about him how God used him AS A HOMOSEXUAL.

Now Lou Engle (one of the leaders of the Awaken the Dawn, and other LOVE movements) is trying to relate this new movement and revival coming to LONNIE FRISBEE. #TheSend is of the devil! #FALSELOVE #ANOTHERJESUS

PEOPLE RUN FROM THIS MESS! WHAT THE WORLD! WAKE UP!

Do you see the ecumenical fangs? People...THIS IS GROSS! How people cannot see what is happening here. THIS NEW LOVE IS NOT OF GOD!

Per the movie's website:

"Frisbee" recounts the life of a radical hippie turned Christian evangelist whose call into the ministry came while involved in the Laguna Beach homosexual scene. Even though he was the spark who propelled two of the largest evangelical denominations in the last thirty years into existence, he was treated with contempt throughout his career because of his sexuality. What do you do when the Jesus freak who starts your church dies from AIDS? Simple. Erase him from history.

Check this out about the movie and promotion of immorality in ministry - http://www.lonniefrisbee.com/. PER LOU ENGLE HIMSELF!

God is inviting us to see one another according to our heavenly calling and destiny and not according to our past or present behavior. When we see Christ clearly, we begin to see ourselves and others differently. Let us say what heaven says about others, releasing revelation and faith into their hearts.

Then, grace can come to empower transfiguration. The Frisbees are flying once again over the West Coast!

PRAYER:

God, this is my prayer, that you would forgive us of our doctrinal policing. Scrutinizing our brother according to the flesh and accusing one another when the days of harvest are at hand. God, raise up harvesters of every kind. Lord, help us to see the treasures in the next wave of the Jesus Movement and not judge them according to their appearances.

We ask forgiveness that so many missed the Jesus Movement because they couldn't see beyond their own cultural lenses. Don't let this happen again in California. Raise up the Lonnie Frisbees. Heal them and let them fly in Jesus Name.

Lou Engle

https://www.facebook.com/notes/thecall/day-17-hidden-treasure-lou-engle/10155790238094902/

I am literally ready to THROW UP! GROSS ME OUT! Notice how Lou says, "doctrinal policing'. PAH-LEASE! RAISE UP LONNIE FRISBEES? GOD HELP THE CHURCH!

The sad thing is that Lou Engle has now partnered with my friends who champion being free from homosexuality. I tried to warn them.

Last Thoughts About NAR

I could literally write a whole book on the New Apostolic Reformation leaders. This book is already too long so I'll just round it up here. According to my research, they've all been planning this since the 80s and maybe before. Many of the leaders were infected by the Kundalini spirit at the so-called Canadian revival called *The Toronto Blessing* – led by Randy Arnott.

The thing about this crazy revival and impartation is that it began in 1994 at the Toronto Airport Vineyard Church (Lonnie Frisbee roots). Out of this strange manifestation event (barking like dogs, etc), came ministries such as Bill Johnson, Mike Bickle, Heidi Baker, Che Ahn, and many more.

The root of NAR stems down to William Branham. Here is a little history on William:

As a young man in the 1950s, Cain toured the country with William Branham, the Pentecostal pioneer of the so-called Post-War Healing Revival – a movement also associated with Oral Roberts and Gordon Lindsay. Branham's ministry was characterised by angelic visions, prophecies and 'words of knowledge' about specific individual healings and life-circumstances. Although aligned to the 'Oneness' tradition of Pentecostalism, which disavowed the trinity and insisted on baptism in the name of Jesus only, Branham appealed to a wider range of Pentecostals thanks to his support for the 'prosperity' teaching of Kenneth Hagin, and to backing from the influential *Full Gospel Business Men's Fellowship*.

Despite his popular profile, Branham went on to promote more controversial doctrines, which came to be regarded by many as heretical.

These included the teaching that Eve's sin involved sexual relations with the serpent in Eden, so that those descended from this 'serpent's seed' were predestined for hell, while others, who had benefited from Branham's ministry, were those predestined to become the bride of Christ. In this scenario, Branham allowed that certain others might through their own freewill be saved out of denominational churches, but that they would have to pass through the Great Tribulation. Denominationalism itself, however, was the 'mark of the beast' (Rev. 13:17). Branham also declared himself to be the angel of Revelation 3:14 and 10:7, and predicted that by 1977 all denominations would be assumed into a World Council of Churches controlled by Rome. (Hilborn, 2000)

Jer 23:16 Thus saith the Lord of hosts, Hearken not unto the words of the prophets that prophesy unto you: they make you vain: they speak a vision of their own heart, and not out of the mouth of the Lord.

Ezekiel 13:1-9 And the word of the Lord came unto me, saying, Son of man, prophesy against the prophets of Israel that prophesy, and say thou unto them that prophesy out of their own hearts. Hear ye the word of the Lord; Thus said the Lord God; Woe unto the foolish prophets, that follow their own spirit, and have seen nothing! O Israel, thy prophets are like the foxes in the deserts. Ye have not gone up into the gaps, neither made up the hedge for the house of Israel to stand in the battle in the day of the Lord. They have seen vanity and lying divination, saying, The Lord saith: and the Lord hath not sent them: and they have made others to hope that they would confirm the word. Have ye not seen a vain vision, and have ye not spoke a lying divination, whereas ye say, The Lord saith it; albeit I have not spoken? Therefore thus saith the Lord God; Because ye have spoken vanity, and seen lies, therefore, behold, I am against you, saith the Lord God. And mine hand shall be upon the prophets that see vanity, and that divine lies: they shall not be in the assembly of my people, neither shall they be written in the writing of the house of the Israel, neither shall they enter into the land of Israel; and ye shall know that I am the Lord God.

Hear my heart church, I am Pentecostal. I am spirit-filled. I came from all of this. I am not denouncing that God gives spiritual gifts. I'm only reporting the root of the modern-day apostasy. Many of the very preachers who went after the "more revelation, power, visitations, experiences, etc", are the ones who in the end went way too far and turned the church over to the Antichrist. They went after the wrong tree and took us to the deep end.

WE MUST COME OUT.

Dr. June Dawn Knight

6

Emergent Church

Remember when I told you how the powers-that-be use both sides of the right and left to achieve their goals. The Emergent Church is the left side of the church. NAR is the right side. (Like Democrats are left and Republicans are right). The NAR reaches a certain demographic of the church, and the left progressive liberals reach the more worldly Christians.

When I think of the Emergent Church (EC), it makes me want to throw up. This is the mixing to the hilt. I can only imagine how God feels about this. Remember I told you that this group waters down the gospel and tries very hard not to offend people. Through this effort, they do not "preach" to the people. They merely have couches all around and the speaker (leader) sits in the middle of the room and hosts discussions. There are no absolutes. Everything is accepted and tolerated. They mix various types of religion into their services. They are all about reaching every one of your senses. (smell, sight, ear, touch, etc.).

This group operates out of the Kundalini spirit as well. If you watch videos of their services, etc., you see that same manifestation. Once you have discernment, you can see this spirit on people. They are a lot like the spirit on New Agers.

This hippie-type look (some call it goofy) ...but it's where they're like in a bliss of the wrong kind. Study it for yourself. Let's see how others describe the EC:

According to author E.M. Bounds (who is very famous for his prayer books), he describes, "There are two ways of directing the church: God's way and the Devil's way. God's way and man's way of running the church are entirely opposite. Man's wise plans, thoughtful resources, and easy solutions are Satan's devices. The Cross is retired and the world comes in. Self-denial is eliminated, and all seems bright, cheerful, and prosperous. Satan's hand is on the controls, and men's schemes prevail. But the church fails under these devices of men.." (Bounds, 1984)

Bride, this book was written in 1984. It's like he's describing the current day church! They have no boundaries in their religion. They mix Buddhism in with New Age in with Occult, Catholism, etc.

The difference between EC and the NAR is that the Emergent Church is more open about their unity goals. NAR hides it. They intentionally deceive the masses. They do meetings behind closed doors to hide their intentions. The Emergent Church is more bold about it. However, they are both rooted in the Catholic Church, one-world-order agenda. **They are together.**

What is the History of the Emergent Church?

According to CBN.com's article explaining what the EC is, "As its name suggests, the emerging church largely consists of Christians involved (or previously involved) in mainstream evangelical churches that have "emerged" from preexisting ideologies and church structures.

Though its current form most likely dates back about 10 years, beginning with a series of leadership conferences and books that were released around that time, the roots of a Christian movement with an emphasis on community, redefining the church experience, cultural application of faith and general discontentment with the evangelical status-quo have even been traced back to the Jesus Movement of 1970s. But the emerging church, as it is known today, first began to surface once again on the mainstream radar after several memoir-style books started garnering attention in the late '90s." (Carey, 2018)

Doug Pagitt, one of the original founders explains about why he helped to start the Emergent Church, "I just don't believe in Christianity anymore. At least not the version of Christianity that has prevailed over the past 1500 years. It just seems to be that there was a version of Christianity that was for that time and that place and they addressed issues that were paramount to those people. Those articulations, not only do they not work today, but frankly they get in the way of the kind of Christianity that we want to have. This kind of Christianity doesn't shut its eyes to any of questions people have today. The kind of Christianity that doesn't go to the past to find its validation." (Pagitt, 2018)

HOPE-FILLED, OPEN-ARMED, ALIVE-AND-WELL FAITH

He explained all of this on his promotional video or his new book about his life story. On the front of his cover he has a cross the is cut off at the top with a flower on it and on the horizontal wood he has arrows on each end.

After watching the video on this website, I tell you what I see. I see where he's cut off the vertical relationship with God (in video he talks about it being an antiquated faith and too old for this generation). So, he's cutting the vertical short and placing a flower arrangement on the top to represent a funeral. This is like a set of funeral flowers on top representing the history of the vertical.

Also, vertical represents the individual relationship with God. Remember I revealed how the ecumenical movement wants to do away with individualistic relationship and go to universal. It's universalist thinking. We should be more concerned about the "kingdom" and the "universal team" or "community" than to be individualistic with God. We should care about the "common good". He also has a place on his website focused on the "Common Good Christians community". He has a network of people where they basically hate on the traditional church. Does this sound like NAR with their reformation? Yes!! Do away with the old church and bring a new order.

Going back to the picture. The picture also represents how they are "social" by the arrows. They want a horizontal relationship with people.

This is also humanistic in thinking because it centers the religion they are creating more around humanity and the NOW than it does the upward vertical relationship to God. It's killing the cross that is meant for Jesus alone and now placing humans on it to be worshipped. Without the cross and the shedding of Jesus' blood, your religion is vanity. It is of none affect.

• HOPE FILLED means that the old religion is full of hatred and white supremacy. It's antiquated and outdated. It's full of gloom and doom and not relevant to today's times.

• OPEN-ARMED means they are inclusive and welcoming of all faiths, religions and people. Well this is what he says about his new network called GREATER THINGS on his website, "GREATER THINGS MAKES CHANGE BY HELPING FAITH LEADERS AND INDIVIDUALS LEAVE BEHIND THE NARRATIVES OF EXCLUSION, VIOLENCE, GREED, SEXISM, EXPLOITATION AND RACISM ROOTED IN WHITE SUPREMACY, AND EMBRACE INSTEAD NEW NARRATIVES OF

RECONCILIATION, INCLUSION, NONVIOLENCE, GENEROSITY, EQUALITY, AND SUSTAINABILITY.

• ALIVE AND WELL FAITH – this means that the old Christianity is a thing of the past. It's dead. Let's put the funeral flowers on top of the cut-off cross. His version of Christianity is the more relevant for the postmodern world.

His Greater Things foundation is to also form a bad name on the word "Christianity". It's all the enemy Bride preparing them for this one-world religion. This group has combined all the religions and still say THEY WORSHIP JESUS! You will learn that there is the true Jesus and a false one.

The Bible warns us about Another Jesus:

2 Corinthians 11:4 For if he that cometh preacheth another Jesus, whom we have not preached, or if ye receive another spirit, which ye have not received, or another gospel, which ye have not accepted, ye might well bear with him.

What Do They Believe?

Pushing the Kingdom – As Above – So Below

On CBN.com's website, this article explains what one of their key leaders says on this subject, "McLaren suggested that Christians should be more focused the prayer of 'thy Kingdom come'— bringing God's Kingdom to Earth through caring for the poor, loving our neighbors and encouraging fellow Christians to grow deeper in their faith, a line of thinking associated with thinkers like Dallas Willard, Tony Campolo and other emerging leaders (Carey, 2018)

I want to point out that notice how they're using social justice to justify "kingdom". I submit to you Bride that all these people in the Ecumenical Movement that are stressing "kingdom" is to build up for the One World Religion. The kingdom they are setting up is for the Antichrist – universalist Jesus.

We discuss this later, but God designed us to evangelize people, not systems. They are all wanting to change THE KINGDOM OF THIS WORLD. The Kingdom of God is WITHIN us. Don't forget that. @ When we evangelize, we are changing people and converting them to Christ. We are taking them out of this world and taking them to the Kingdom of God. We're doing that in the heart, not in the Earth.

Partnering with the Pope's Missional Purpose and Plans Ecumenical "Conversation" is one of the emerging church's most well- known buzzwords. Like-minded leaders began to engage other churches and leaders in topics like those McLaren had been writing about.

Pastors like Doug Pagitt, Tony Jones and Rob Bell started putting the ideas—the importance of community, "missional" living (another emerging buzzword that describes the act of using people's cultural understanding to reach them with the gospel) and open discussion—into practice. (Carey, 2018)

As I explained in the Ecumenical section of this book, the Emergent Church is a part of the Pope's plans to setup social justice activities all over the world. This is how they are all "coming together" in unity. It's a false unity based upon social justice. They leave their doctrine at the door and only go to help humanity's immediate need.

Well, the EC (Emergent Church) leaders are Pope-puppets for the bigger picture of later taking over the world. Let's look at some other leader's positions on their mission's programs.

They are changing the word "Christian" to "Kingdom" because they want to get away from individuality and become community – universalism – plurality – thus kingdom. Look at what one of the leaders of the Emergent Church says on his website about this, "The American church today suffers from a self-inflicted problem: preaching a 'divided' gospel that emphasizes individualistic salvation in Christ over against the larger overall message of the Kingdom of God. The primary theme of the entire New Testament is the Kingdom of God with all its societal and cultural implications, a theme clearly seen in the preaching of John the Baptist, Jesus, and the apostle Paul." (Mattera, 2017)

This ecumenical movement wants to do away with the separatist fundamentalist Christianity that believes in the word of God literally and evangelical where we do missions for souls of individual people. They are equating kingdom to the SYSTEM.

It's a humanistic approach to change the outside world. In the Bible the only kingdom that will be setup next in our lifetime is the Antichrist about to step on the scene which I will discuss later.

Apostasy's Motive Straight from a Demon

I saw a post on Facebook where they said that they found a video they recorded of a revival at so and so's church and they wanted everyone to enjoy it. My radar went up because this church is one of the head ones of the Emergent Church. (God's been leading me to keys in my research. I knew this was a key).

So, as I'm watching this unbelievable service, I transcribed some of what was said. This man had the microphone and was prophesying. It was so demonic! After hearing it I realized this was the real demon exposing his motives! I have the proof of this on video. Is this not creepy? Let me point out a few things. I will comment in black:

I bless the rising (the crazy sounds) of the tide of the GREATER GLORY WITHIN EVERYONE'S BELLY tonight. (Rising of the Kundalini serpent spirit). Can you do a prophetic act and open up the gates to the prophetic in your life tonight (Demon needed everyone to come in agreement with its call)

((demonic sounds)) We doubled our dare (You can tell this is not God. We do not double-dog-dare God for anything. We do not have any authority for that period!) for the glory of the King to come forth and not behave (This king is the prince of darkness. Not Behave? This says it all!) and set us ablaze. We call in the river of fire. The fire and the wind. (Earth, wind and fire are the elements of witchcraft)

Up from the belly he arose. (Belly of the Earth the Beast shall arise basically). Let the sound of the arisen (The Beast's sound?) come and ruin everything of religion. (This is all-out war on Christianity).

Ruin everything that we think of church, (Christianity), every argument and speculation of what we know of God. (Bring mass confusion?) Ruin us again God. That solid feeling that we feel when we leave here (Fulness of Satan), will multiply and become one voice (come together in Christ-Consciousness as one in the universe). (Satanic voice) as one body as one drink. (One Body is in Unity of this Drunken Apostasy). You are unifying one body that cannot be unified by doctrine and religion.

(This right here told what this is. It is spirit of antichrist speaking. It is declaring that it doesn't want anything to do with truth and doctrine!) It's being born in this place to reveal the face of the beloved son. (The devil, the beast. The son is not the one we think of with Jesus. It means Satan. When it says 'reveal the face' I think of the morning star – Lucifer means morning star – angel of light. He mimics.)

There is much more on this video, but I wanted you to see the point of it. It was very demonic with growling sounds and creepy contortions on this man. Ugh. I think it revealed what this spirit thinks. I also think it may be Cain. The Spirit of Cain is angry and a murderer. It's also jealous of his brother. Just keep your eyes out Bride. Be wise and alert. There is some crazy stuff going on out there!

Final Thoughts About NAR & Emergent Church
The Family

There is a series on Netflix called *The Family*. It's made up of five (5) shows. It is extremely eye-opening. Before I watched this movie I could not understand how the NAR preachers could partner with the LGBTQ agenda and other religions and not have a conscience about it.

However, after this movie it explains it. It's actually not a movie, it's a documentary about a man who lived in this elitism Washington DC club house of the evangelicals.

These men ran the world using the name of "Jesus". They said that everything will be ok in the group as long as you said the name of Jesus. They do not care if you murder, rape, or anything else as long as you say that name. This explained it to me that they are deceptive and wicked. They think if they can get you to come in agreement with them and their sin by just saying that name that you are now in a pact with them. I encourage you to watch the documentary.

7

The Great
Deception/Apostasy

I pray that by the time you reached this chapter that you realize what it is. It is the stage being set for the one world order, the one world church, the "community", and the global "oneness" coming together. The deception is that the truth is not being preached. However, for you that took the time to read this book, it is being revealed to you so that you can make right decisions accordingly. This is what the word says,

> *2 Timothy 2:15 Study to shew thyself approved unto God, a workman that needeth not to be ashamed, rightly dividing the word of truth.*

We are going to look at what the word says about this and examine it with what is taking place on the Earth today. First, let me make it very clear, this great awakening, great Utopia, peace and unity days ahead are NOT FOR THE CHRISTIANS. This is terminology for the one world system.

This is the only peace that is going to come is a fake peace. The Bible has already foretold it. You will barely hear the ministers involved with the Ecumenical Movement (EM), New Apostolic Reformation (NAR), or Emergent Church (EC) describe their end-time beliefs. Most of them avoid it or do not mention it at all. We will examine this more.

You must ask yourself why all these people spend more time talking about signs, miracles and wonders, kingdom, blessings, etc., instead of preaching about Hell, sin, judgment coming, end of times, Book of Revelation, etc. Why? The New Testament writers spend more time warning people than blessing people. Why are they not talking about the very thing (sin) that will keep them away from God? Isn't this strange?

I believe that while Trump is president, that it gives the remnant the chance to repent and setup/prepare for what is coming. I still believe that he is a part of the globalist UN plan and he has pulled the evangelicals in long before he ran for office. This is why Paula White lived in Trump Towers. I believe they planned all this out. Trump is not Superman. He cannot accomplish all this by himself. Although he likes to take credit for all of it, he cannot do it. It's the whole system at work. So, while he and the media is keeping us distracted about him and his wars, the Beast system is being setup. It's coming together at rapid speed. However, at the MOMENT it seems as though the church has a moment of peace. Believe me...the worst is yet to come.

What we see happening in Washington DC is a prelude to what is coming to the church. We will see great exposure and the filth/vomit will be revealed so that people may get their eyes back on God and repent for their compromising and mixture.

While they are screaming PEACE…we must be thankful for this moment of sunshine because we have a great storm on the horizon. It's all because of the apostasy and the lukewarm church. She has cheated on God.

How Does the Bible Describe the Apostasy?

The Bible talks about false prophets in the last days, the great deception, the apostasy more than it does many things. See the scriptures:

> *1 Timothy 4: 1-16 - 1 Now the Spirit speaketh expressly, that in the latter times some shall depart from the faith, giving heed to seducing spirits, and doctrines of devils; 2 Speaking lies in hypocrisy; having their conscience seared with a hot iron; 3 Forbidding to marry, and commanding to abstain from meats, which God hath created to be received with thanksgiving of them which believe and know the truth. 4 For every creature of God is good, and nothing to be refused, if it be received with thanksgiving: 5 For it is sanctified by the word of God and prayer. 6 If thou put the brethren in remembrance of these things, thou shalt be a good minister of Jesus Christ, nourished up in the words of faith and of good doctrine, whereunto thou hast attained. 7 But refuse profane and old wives' fables, and exercise thyself rather unto godliness. 8 For bodily exercise profiteth little: but godliness is profitable unto all things, having promise of the life that now is, and of that which is to come.*

9 This is a faithful saying and worthy of all acceptation. 10 For therefore we both labour and suffer reproach, because we trust in the living God, who is the Saviour of all men, specially of those that believe. 11 These things command and teach. 12 Let no man despise thy youth; but be thou an example of the believers, in word, in conversation, in charity, in spirit, in faith, in purity. 13 Till I come, give attendance to reading, to exhortation, to doctrine. 14 Neglect not the gift that is in thee, which was given thee by prophecy, with the laying on of the hands of the presbytery. 15 Meditate upon these things; give thyself wholly to them; that thy profiting may appear to all. 16 Take heed unto thyself, and unto the doctrine; continue in them: for in doing this thou shalt both save thyself, and them that hear thee.

Matthew 7:15 Beware of false prophets, which come to you in sheep's clothing, but inwardly they are ravening wolves.

Matthew 24:11 And many false prophets shall rise, and shall deceive many.

Matthew 24:24 For there shall arise false Christs, and false prophets, and shall shew great signs and wonders; insomuch that, if it were possible, they shall deceive the very elect.

Mark 13:22 For false Christs and false prophets shall rise, and shall shew signs and wonders, to seduce, if it were possible, even the elect.

Luke 6:26 Woe unto you, when all men shall speak well of you! for so did their fathers to the false prophets.

2 Peter 2:1 But there were false prophets also among the people, even as there shall be false teachers among you, who privily shall bring in damnable heresies, even denying the Lord that bought them, and bring upon themselves swift destruction.

1 John 4:1 Beloved, believe not every spirit, but try the spirits whether they are of God: because many false prophets are gone out into the world.

The Bible also talks about the condition of the church in the last days. Tell me if it says anything about a glorious church rising to take over the world full of power and glory and a great Utopia is coming through the seven-mountain mandate, etc. Also, see if it tells you that through partnering with unholy matrimonies that it will bring the power of God onto people in the last days.

1 Timothy 3:1-17 - 1 This know also, that in the last days perilous times shall come.

2 For men shall be lovers of their own selves, covetous, boasters, proud, blasphemers, disobedient to parents, unthankful, unholy, 3 Without natural affection, trucebreakers, false accusers, incontinent, fierce, despisers of those that are good, 4 Traitors, heady, highminded, lovers of pleasures more than lovers of God; 5 Having a form of godliness, but denying the power thereof: from such turn away. 6 For of this sort are they which creep into houses, and lead captive silly women laden with sins, led away with divers lusts,7 Ever learning, and never able to come to the knowledge of the truth. 8 Now as Jannes and Jambres withstood Moses, so do these also resist the truth: men of corrupt minds, reprobate concerning the faith. 9 But they shall proceed no further: for their folly shall be manifest unto all men, as their's also was. 10 But thou hast fully known my doctrine, manner of life, purpose, faith, longsuffering, charity, patience, 11 Persecutions, afflictions, which came unto me at Antioch, at Iconium, at Lystra; what persecutions I endured: but out of them all the Lord delivered me. 12 Yea, and all that will live godly in Christ Jesus shall suffer persecution. 13 But evil men and seducers shall wax worse and worse, deceiving, and being deceived. 14 But continue thou in the things which thou hast learned and hast been assured of, knowing of whom thou hast learned them;

15 And that from a child thou hast known the holy scriptures, which are able to make thee wise unto salvation through faith which is in Christ Jesus. 16 All scripture is given by inspiration of God, and is profitable for doctrine, for reproof, for correction, for instruction in righteousness: 17 That the man of God may be perfect, thoroughly furnished unto all good works.

James 5:1-10 - 1Go to now, ye rich men, weep and howl for your miseries that shall come upon you. 2 Your riches are corrupted, and your garments are motheaten. 3 Your gold and silver is cankered; and the rust of them shall be a witness against you, and shall eat your flesh as it were fire. Ye have heaped treasure together for the last days. 4 Behold, the hire of the labourers who have reaped down your fields, which is of you kept back by fraud, crieth: and the cries of them which have reaped are entered into the ears of the Lord of sabaoth. 5 Ye have lived in pleasure on the Earth, and been wanton; ye have nourished your hearts, as in a day of slaughter. 6 Ye have condemned and killed the just; and he doth not resist you. 7 Be patient therefore, brethren, unto the coming of the Lord. Behold, the husbandman waiteth for the precious fruit of the Earth, and hath long patience for it, until he receive the early and latter rain. 8 Be ye also patient; stablish your hearts: for the coming of the Lord draweth nigh. 9 Grudge not one against another, brethren, lest ye be condemned: behold, the judge standeth before the door.

10 Take, my brethren, the prophets, who have spoken in the name of the Lord, for an example of suffering affliction, and of patience.

As you can tell by these scriptures, there is the message that the Earth will be in great distress and like the days of Noah. Terrible days and therefore we must not allow the spirit of the world to infiltrate us. We must remain pure, holy and consecrated to the Lord. Do not touch the unclean thing and separate from the apostasy. You will learn in T*he American Judgment* book when God brings judgment, everyone attached to that apostasy will get judged!

Ecumenical Movement Explained by Roger Oakland

Ecumenical and unbiblical teachings are being endorsed for the cause of unity and church growth. The Gospel of Jesus Christ is being disguised to make it less offensive and more acceptable.

Churches that once taught the Bible faithfully verse by verse preparing the flock for the imminent return of Jesus Christ, now are looking for ways to make their services more seeker-friendly and are less concerned about the prophetic signs we are living in the last days.

Pastors and churches that once believed church growth was dependent on feeding the sheep and equipping the saved to share the Gospel, now promote humanistic means to draw in the masses based on a consumer style of evangelism focused on "finding out what people want" to "get them in the door."

Churches once led by pastors committed to biblical truth, now are employing experts who use worldly principles borrowed from secular corporations with material goals for success.

Rather than following Jesus and His Word, pastors and church leaders are looking to successful men and their methods so they can become part of a movement that is based on principles foreign to the Scriptures.

When church leaders promoting strategies to establish the Kingdom of God here on earth by humanistic methods are challenged by concerned believers warning about the dangers, the leaders label these believers as divisive. Contending for the faith is no longer considered biblical. A person taking a position for biblical truth is now accused of being critical of what others believe.

Bible-believing pastors who once taught the Bible are now looking for ways to attract people to their congregations by providing extra-biblical experiences [e.g. contemplative] and an atmosphere that includes candles, icons, incense, and the introduction of Roman Catholic sacraments. When concerned observers suggest this appears to be leading to a partnership with Roman Catholicism, they are considered to be negative opponents of the "new thing" God is doing to reach our generation. (Oakland R. , 2012)

Major Ecumenical Events & Catholic Church

Bride keep your eye out for big events because they are all in this together. They are increasing more and more today. Do you notice how it's the same ones partnering together? It's because of the big picture. They are partnering more with the Catholic Church at these events. If you know they're ecumenical then run.

They all are in a network and they sign off on each other's books, preach at each other's churches, and meet at these conferences. It's a billion-dollar industry! They are making merchandise out of you.

I'm not against coming together in unity...however, I am against partnering with the apostasy. God hates mixing.

Burning Man & Wild Goose Festival
Wild Goose Festival

This festival is Emergent Church on steroids. It is a love-fest of the future. This is where this ecumenical movement and all this is leading to. It is an interfaith movement festival and the building of a new church (the one world church).

See what their website says about it...

It's transformational, experiential, it's a sing and dance and play and dream and eat and camp and meditate and talk and listen and twirl-you-around-and-shake-you-up gathering, born out of the "Wild Goose" spirit metaphor which is all about beauty, grace, and yes, unpredictability.

We also take inspiration from events such as, Greenbelt, **Burning Man**, *Lightning In a Bottle and SXSW.*

It is a place where all are welcome. Seriously, ALL. Because we are rooted in a progressive Christian tradition, we welcome you, whatever your age, race, culture, gender, marital status, sexual orientation, religious tradition, disabilities, different abilities, whether you have money or not, whether you have a degree or not, whether you have a strong faith or no faith, or perhaps a billion questions about faith, whether you have a home or not, whether you're an extrovert or introvert, everyone is welcome here.

Even eye-rolling teenagers. And rambunctious little kids. Rambunctiousness is, in fact, encouraged. We welcome all to come and seek the common good together." (Wild Goose Festival, 2016)

Notice how they use the key words, "common good". This tells you the Pope is behind this. I also want you to notice Bride how they said this is partnered with *The Burning Man* festival.

This is a Satanic Ritual festival! Ugh! This thing gets so deep. However, the Luciferians are behind Illuminati and Jesuits anyway, so it is all antichrist spirit. Notice as well that it is an inclusive event of all religions. This is that interfaith movement.

You'll be shocked to learn who the speakers are this year (2018). The usual EC speakers such as Brian McClaren, Doug Pagitt, but also Amy Grant. This grieves me.

An article written on Tony Jones' website (he's another EC speaker/leader) about the Wild Goose Festival and the Eucharist, "Last year at the Wild Goose Festival, the band, The Liturgists, hosted a worship experience one night, which culminated in communion. I was among several people invited to help serve. As each person came forward and stood in front of me, I tore off a small piece of bread, dipped it into a cup of wine, and offered it, along with the words many people say as a part of this church sacrament, 'The body of Christ, broken for you. The blood of Christ, shed for you.'" She continues explaining why her doubt and disdain for those words cause her to want to operate in more love by stating the following, "Christ is here, in your brokenness - Christ is here, bringing you to life"., (Rand, 2016)

She's talking about wanting to change the traditional words. Notice the word "Christ" which means universal – Christ-Consciousness.

167

Hillsong Alpha Conference 2018

Hillsong has been doing some crazy stuff these past few years. Watch the video of their newest release called *PEACE*. It is eerie and freaky! People that watched it are providing strange responses.

I'll tell you mine. It is like the video of the Great Whore of Babylon rising. It displays a bride in red with a bunch of brides in white on the floor with crowns on their head. As this whore walks through the white brides, the crowns come off. It's very dark and sinister. The spirit behind the video is sinister.

Then the Alpha conference I see they have the Catholic Church up there doing the Eucharist with the people! So…it's setting up for the false kingdom.

This is on their website advertising for that Alpha Conference:

Culture is shifting.

Only 2 in 10 Americans under 30 believe attending church is important or worthwhile (an all-time low).

59 percent of millennials raised in a church have dropped out. 35 percent of millennials have an anti-church stance, believing

the church does more harm than good. [Barna]

This is more than a problem; this is an opportunity. What if the church finds a way forward? What if this shift represents the soil for spiritual renewal?

What if the kingdom of God can break into our new post-Christian reality on Earth as it is in heaven?

At The Alpha Conference 2018 we will explore this question: how can we cultivate a kingdom culture within the local church?

A culture of unexpected hospitality and grace that breaks down barriers to the gospel. A culture of deepening dependence on prayer and expectancy on God's Spirit.

A culture that builds unity across historical church divides. (Hillsong, 2018)

Notice how this description on their website says, "post Christian". This is what I'm trying to tell you. They are shifting from "Christian" culture to "Kingdom". Christian = individual (vertical) between you and God.

Kingdom = horizontal which represents universalism and relationships with humans. The example I gave about EC's Doug Pagitt's book with the top of the cross cutoff is a perfect example of this. They are killing the individualism of us and God and going global - Christ-Consciousness.

Terminology of the Ecumenical Movement/Apostasy

This movement is changing the way we define everything. I'm going to break this down very clearly from my research the way I'm interpreting all this. You can go through this book and to the back of the Works Cited page to get all the proof. This is my interpretation of their shenanigans:

EM Terms vs True Church Christianity Terms

EM Terms	True Christianity Terms
Body of Christ - Means one collective body of humanity to come together in one Christ-Consciousness awareness that we are to build a Tower of Babel and a new Earth.	The Bride of Christ, the church – the remnant. This is God's children on the Earth. This does NOT include everyone. Only the ones who confess that Jesus is the ONLY way to Heaven
Kingdom – This kingdom is made up of the seven-mountain mandate. The end goal is to missionize the world for the Pope. We are all coming together in unity to pull everyone together for the Christ-Consciousness and the One World Religion/Church. This kingdom means universe – outward and to create Kingdom Now. Utopia on the Earth of peace and brotherhood. We teach them that suffering is not of God. Christians are the only ones in our way in this kingdom. We do not like the old order.	Kingdom on this side means that it is the Kingdom of Heaven. This is inside each Christian. When we evangelize the world, it means humans (souls). We are evangelizing people not to raise them up to take over the world and to partner with ungodly associations, but to teach them. they must serve and obey God. Kingdom is on the inside of each of the children of God. They are operating out of that kingdom's authority, but don't use that authority to override God's will.

We speak against the word "Christianity" and "Traditional way of Protestant Churches now". We want to reform the whole system to this new Earth and world where it's all ran by superpowers of elitists labeled as apostles and prophets. We are not "servants" to God. We are equal to him and gods our self. Therefore, we can go to the courts of heaven and fight for yourself and do contemplative prayer and other forms to control our own destiny.	They understand that God has written what is to come. They also understand that we will suffer when we speak truth, thus they prepare humanity for the end of days and to make the right choice. When the Antichrist steps on the scene and wants them all to take a mark in their right hands and on their forehead declaring the mark of the beast, they will not do it. We are servants not masters
Communion In this side the communion is either involving the Eucharist now or headed that way. We are inclusive and have the beauty and love of god. (The Eucharist is worshipping an idol which is forbidden by God.) We believe the priest has the authority to turn the Eucharist into Jesus.	We do communion by a cracker and grape juice as a representative of Christ. We believe communion is a time of repentance and remembrance. It's a time of reflection of our sins and condition of our heart before God. We take it very seriously.

Love –	
We have the real love because we are not judgmental. We're tolerant, inclusive, accepting and love mixing all religions together to form one melting pot of love. It's a New Age Love. We are AS ONE. We blend with other religions. The fundamentalists are haters and bigots. They are also "spiritual terrorists". Therefore, we will end up killing them in the end so that we can continue and have our great Utopia.	We believe that Jesus is love. Jesus did not put up with sin and greed. He turned the tables in the temple because he couldn't stand corruption, yet he loved. True love tells the truth. It is not politically correct. It is not passive. It is passionate about God's heart towards sin and obedience. The only reason the other side feels that this side is harsh is because this side sticks by the word of God. The truth hurts, but it sets you free.
Jesus –	
This is Another Jesus. We say the words, but it does not mean the one that is your God.	The Jesus on this side came to fulfill the law, not extend grace to excuse sin. This Jesus is holy and spoke what he heard his father say. God's heart is holy and righteous. Jesus came to transform people and set them free. His desire is not that they stay in their sin, but that they get set free and become the identity that He has for them.
This is Another Jesus that the Bible warned you about. We tell people sin no longer bothers them because Jesus paid it all on the cross. The Tree of Knowledge no longer exists. However, our truth supersedes your truth because it is humanism.	

Because the universe says that this Jesus is the real love, this is the one we're sticking by. Everyone is included. It doesn't matter your sin, Jesus understands. Sin doesn't bother you anymore. Just say the name of Jesus and continue in your sin. You are like David and others who sinned but God still used them. This Jesus accepts you just as you are and don't worry about changing. This Jesus there is no consequences because there is no sin. It's all relative.

This Jesus has expectations. He says he must know that you love him more than you do your own family or possessions. This Jesus will cost you everything. This Jesus corrects you and rebukes you. This Jesus has consequences.

This Jesus will cost you everything. He requires holiness and not to touch the unclean thing.

Faith –

EM requires NO FAITH. We are very haughty. We need the extra and think we know it all. There are many ways to get to Heaven. We have figured it all out - Good and Evil. We either do not need the Bible because we have the spirit or we use the Bible to say what we want it to say. We seek for more.

Although we may doubt and question God sometimes, it requires that we trust God in all things. We pray, obey and trust.

This faith requires that we may not see or know what's ahead and we truth God as we follow his voice. It's a blind faith. He leads and we follow.

We say supernatural knowledge. the ways NAR and EC are with His word, and trust Him. We throw God out the window.

We do it our way through Contemplative Prayer, Courts of Heaven, Centering Prayer Meditation (Eastern Way), of heaven and astral-project our souls out of our bodies,

Yoga, holistic, Essential Oils, Liturgy, Eucharist, Grave-Soaking, Destiny Cards masqueraded as Tarot Cards, Crystals, Positivity, Energy, Healings, Life Coaching, Empowerment Speaking, inner-god healing, gems, gold dust, feathers, SOZO, homosexuals to preach, etc. We do not need faith (unless its faith within ourselves and universe).

Mixing with the World UNITY	
This side is uniting all religions and faiths & form one church. This is universal in nature.	We do not believe in unity at the cost of doctrine. We must be in unity at the agreement of foundational truths of the Bible. The Bride of Christ is the remnant and that is who we partner with. Not other faiths, religions, doctrines against the word, the world, etc.

There's many more, but those just about cover it. I pray you understand now what the apostasy is. When you go to their conferences and events, they're speaking what you want to hear and getting your money at the same time. They're also finding out who are the catalysts in each city. They're wanting to partner in networks with the go-getters so that they can take over your city. You must be sober and alert to recognize it. We need discernment in this hour.

Check out their websites and their statement of beliefs. You will see how most of them adopted the Apostle's Creed and the Nicene Creed which is basically worshipping the Catholic Church as the one holy church. Know who you labor among. Research. They say the word catholic in the creeds mean "universal church", but the language seems plain enough. It means the Catholic Church – which does consider themselves the "mother church", the "universal one church".

EM - Revival Coming

Author Roger Oakland has this same theory about this false revival coming, "I am not certain when I first realized that the Roman Catholic Church, particularly the Jesuits, were the root force behind the coming one-world religion.." (Oakland R. , 2012) He continues, "Through writing New Wine and the Babylonian Vine, I could see that the final one-world religion will be a mix of all religions for the cause of peace.

This will include a revival of ancient Babylonianism that will be rooted in the worship of creation, based on Darwinian evolution that is rooted in Hinduism and Buddhism." Bride, notice how he said it will be a revival of ancient Babylonianism." (Oakland R. , 2012)

The only difference between his theory and mine is that I did not equate it as the Babylonian type. I equate it to a universal, Christ-Consciousness fake revival with the look-alike of ours. The difference will be that this revival will not have true transformation such as repentance and a turning from sin. What they may label as revival may be the same example as the Toronto Blessing outpouring.

Look at the fruit of that revival. The big-named ministers who branched off from it became apostate. Why? What happened there to turn them into a mixture of New Age, Occult, Kundalini and other spirits?

Look at what a former pastor participant said about the Toronto experience;

I laughed at people acting like dogs and pretending to urinate on the columns of the TACF building. I watched people pretend to be animals, bark, roar, cluck, pretend to fly as if they had wings, perpetually act drunk and sing silly songs.

How I thought that any of this was from the Holy Spirit of God amazes me today.

It was loud irreverent and blasphemous to the Holy God of the Bible. I suppose in my mind I reasoned that as long as they did not teach anything in direct violation to scripture then it was what we called the exotic. This is a buzz word for manifestations that could not be justified from a biblical perspective.

I was taught from the pulpit that we had two options. The order of the nursery full of life and messy or the order of the graveyard, very orderly but dead! As a young immature pastor I wanted life with mess. I failed to remember that God wants us to become mature and grow up in him. I became disconcerted by the prophetic words that came forth especially one by Carol Arnott in which she had her bride experience where she was taken into the very presence of Jesus and said that the love that she experienced was even better than sex! I was shocked in my spirit and thought how can one compare the love of God with sex? When we suspected that demons were running riot in our services John Arnott would teach that we should ask are they coming or going. If they are leaving then that is ok!

John would defend the chaos by saying that we ought not be afraid of being deceived, if we have asked the Holy Spirit to come and fill us then how could Satan come and deceive us? This would make Satan very strong and God very weak! He said that we needed to have more faith in a Big God to protect us than in a Big Devil to deceive us. This sounded very convincing but was totally contrary to scripture for Jesus and Paul and Peter and John all warn us about the power of deceiving spirits and especially so in the last days.

Again we did not love God enough to obey His Word and the result was that we opened ourselves up to lying spirits. May God have mercy upon us! (Gowdy, n.d.)

This gentleman/pastor was a Vineyard pastor when this movement began in 1994.

He visited it and now he's writing to the church with a repentant heart about his participation in this heresy. I would like to point out that many of our big-named ministers today ALL GOT THEIR FILLINGS SPIRITUALLY FROM THIS SO- CALLED OUTPOURING.

It was an outpouring alright...but it wasn't holy! Also notice how in his article he describes John Arnott's excuse to continue with the heretical behavior and manifestations during it. According to this man's testimony, the following is the result of that outpouring.

After three years of being in the thick of the Toronto blessing our Vineyard assembly in Scarborough (East Toronto) just about self-destructed. We devoured one another, with gossip, backstabbing, division, sects criticism etc. After three years of 'soaking,' praying for people, shaking, rolling, laughing, roaring, ministering at TACF on their prayer team, leading worship at TACF, preaching at TACF, basically living at TACF we were the most carnal, immature and deceived Christians that I know.

I remember saying to my friend and senior pastor at Scarborough Vineyard Church in 1997 that ever since the Toronto Blessing came we have just about fallen to bits! He agreed! (Gowdy, n.d.)

Of course, this is one pastor's perception and testimony of what happened there, however, you can hear his heart in this article that he is very sorry that he participated in it. I wanted to show you how they had all the manifestations that fooled the thousands that attended but wasn't real lasting change.

This false revival coming may look cool because signs, miracles and wonders are happening, but what fruit will become of it?

I want to encourage all of you readers to be very careful who lays hands on you and speaks over you.

A few signs to watch for to know if it's fake:

• #1 – Is the Pope involved with it

• Are they out there with other mixed beliefs? If so, God can't be in it because He will not mix with heresy or be tainted

• Is the word of God involved – the Bible? Not THEIR version of the Bible…but the King James Version? There's a few versions that are good…but really know.

• Are the lives truly being saved and transformed? What good is a healing (remember many religions can heal AND prophecy) when their soul is going to Hell?

• Are they using the terms "common good" "Christ" (instead of Jesus Christ – but even then, you must pay close attention) "inclusive" "Christ-Consciousness" "Kingdom" "community" "ecumenical" "common" "plurality" "universe" "mother church" "catholic church" "glory-realm", etc.

• Who are they partnering with? Investigate these people

• Are they mixing with worldly people & ideas?

Triangle of Death

In this book we have examined the big picture of what they are doing to infiltrate the church. Now I want to explain it another way. I drew a graph and I want you to see it:

**As Above
So Below**

Kingdom of This World
Kingdom of Hell

**Kingdom
One World
Religion**

No more Vertical
Only Horizontal

all-seeing eye at top

Left/
Progressive

Right/
Conservative

**Emergent
Church**

**Black Liberation
Theology**

Ecumenical

**New Apostolic
Reformation
(NAR)**

Movement

Grace/Hope

No Boundaries to Sin

Extra-Biblical/
Too Much Knowledge

Utopia &
Peace Ahead

Inclusive

Eucharist/
Catholic

New Age &
Occult

Christ-
Consciousness

More Experience
Over Bible & Truth

Pride

No faith & No Bibles

Rome

Not a Servant or
Child to God

Body of Christ
(New Age Style)

Dr. June Knight

Explanation of the Graphic

*The cross is short at the top because they are cutting our
salvation off. They are cutting the vertical way of Christianity
out.*

They are doing away with the 'ole rigid Jesus and his rules/boundaries and going horizontal to relationships where it's humanity and universal!

Vertical = individuality Horizontal = universalism/global

• The triangle represents the Catholic Church being behind all of this. Through them is the Illuminati, Jesuits, etc. (All those that control the narrative in the world). The triangle always represents the Masons, etc.

• Inside the triangle at the roots is the word ROME. This represents where this all stems FROM and where it's all GOING!

• The other words are the root of what they're trying to do – terms they are using and motives of all sides. It's all in this triangle pointing UPWARDS to the one world religion

• The Word ECUMENICAL MOVEMENT is in the middle because it crosses the intersection of the tree you see in the picture. The tree represents AS ABOVE, SO BELOW. Remember that the Earth is Satan's heaven. Hell is Below. You will see this a lot on the logos of this Kingdom movement. This is sinister. This means they're telling all the elite that this is for another reason. So, the EM word is in the middle because it is behind all of this. They say bring Kingdom of Heaven down to earth, but their actions speak otherwise.

• At the top of the tree and the top of the cut-off cross is the words KINGDOM – ONE WORLD RELIGION. This means that this is what this new kingdom will be that they are ALL working towards. When they partner with the Ecumenical Movement, then they are headed towards this big goal.

• On the horizontal lines on one side of the tree is the right and other side is the left. It displays the ones represented in the white section. It's all headed towards the same goal and purpose. Although they are on opposite spectrums, they are speaking the SAME LANGUAGE FOR THE SAME OUTCOME.

Think of the scripture that says, ALL THINGS TO ALL PEOPLE. They are morphing into the various types of people and Christians to pull them towards the same kingdom, which is universalism, plurality and the Christ-consciousness. It's the one world religion - Whore of Babylon.

The circle at the top represents the all-seeing eye at the top of the pyramid – Illuminati.

As you can tell by this graph, they are using OUR terminology against us with totally different outcomes. They do not mean the same thing that we do, or the Bible does. This is the slickest deception ever!

When these ministers partner with this movement, it's like when rock stars a pop stars partner with the Illuminati. It's the same group. When rock stars line up with the beast, they become famous and all doors open. It's the same in this movement. You line up with them and it will advance you. The difference is that you're selling your soul to the devil.

Love Letter from Ecumenical Movement

Hello Catalyst! Come join the ecumenical movement because we are synergizing across the world with all faiths and we want you in our special elite club.

We are coming together more and more through the ecumenical events so that we can find the catalysts in each community (go-getters, leaders). Make sure you tell your friends to come! Then we want to have YOU join our networks, send us money and then we will be your apostle and overseer.

Then, we will make YOU an apostle/leader over a hub/tribe/network. Then as you pull people into this movement, you will send us 10% of your bring-in or a certain amount to us. Then you should bring them to all our meetings, conferences, calls, video conferences, etc. You are required to have a mentor and you are to tell them every move you're making. Don't dare talk about us or you will pay the ultimate price!

Then you should tell your whole community about us so that we can pull them in as well to buy all our books and attend their conferences. We want their soul too!

Then we can taint everyone involved! Then we have set you up like a pyramid scheme. It brings us more money and gets our books/products/network sold in your city. You are our SPECIAL catalyst. It's all about the money and it all goes back to Rome, so don't worry! It's all for the common good. It's "community".

Also, don't forget that most all our leaders have tattoos and look so cool doing their LIVE streaming with them all hanging out then YOU can get one too and build up so much pride and begin to infiltrate your city and everyone that is attached to YOU. Then YOU can take over the seven-mountain-mandate and become a superhero and take over the world. You don't need to be a servant anymore. YOU only need to be on top of the mountain. You only need to be an apostle now! YOU only need to be in the courts of heaven fighting your case astral-projecting out of your body.

Then you need to do contemplative prayer so that you can visualize everything, chant, meditate, and open yourself up to the Kundalini spirit. Then YOU need to use all your dominion super-powers and command the mountains to move outside of God's will. YOU have so much authority that America should not be sick anymore. Now you can bring your new friends to fire tunnels and impart all these spirits into the masses and recruit other people!

You have so much superpower that YOU are now a superhero yourself. YOU no longer need the word of God because it is antiquated. It is written by a bunch of racist and it wasn't even God that wrote that book. DON'T YOU SEE IT? It's no longer relevant for this hour! How dare you!

You don't need faith anymore, all you need is to do contemplative prayer like the old mystics did and the New Agers/Hindus. You can do Yoga and stretch your body towards all the gods. You can do essential oils and put the oils on your temple from God-knows-where. You can follow the advice from other witches and people who have probably cast spells on it. Why not? YOU can even sell them to your church folks and get them involved in New Age. You can even do martial arts in your church. No problem! Just expose everyone there to these spirits! Then why not just do the tarot cards – disguised as destiny cards. Why not just do grave sucking and go to graves to suck their energy up? Why not just do labyrinths and pray mystically?

Why not just speak out against the word "Christianity" and "Christian" and continue promoting "kingdom"? After all, YOU just hate how it's been done for thousands of years and you think you know more than them and the Bible. I mean really. Just do it!

There's nothing holding YOU back in this kingdom. Heck, we don't even believe in Hell! Ha! Pah-lease! We tell you grace and hope and that YOU don't have to worry about sin because Jesus took it all on the cross and he already paid the price!

No! Just keep giving in to your carnality! Christ understands! Notice I said the word Christ? Yes, the universe knows that YOU are ONLY human and not God! Wait a minute, I meant to tell you that you ARE god. Yes with a little g. YOU are little gods running around and we're about to build a tower of Babel again! Yes!

We are going to form this great Utopia in the Earth and take over the world! Wait a minute, there must be a great awakening first! Yes, it's dawning a new day! The dawn that we're talking about is Satan about to take his throne! Yes! You heard me!

The prince of darkness who was Lucifer, he was wrongly done by God and you're going to help him setup his kingdom! We're going to do a massive revival and missions work across the world to help with the common good and social justice! Don't you dare do missions work and try to convert or help people's salvation! No proselytizing! We're only out to build this worldly universe and kingdom! No more are we worried about souls to God! We're more worried about soldiers in this army to help the Pope!

And, don't worry, those Christians you hate so much…you will be able to KILL THEM YOURSELF! We will partner with the Orthodox Jews and bring you under the Noahide Laws! Yes, that spirit of Cain on the inside of YOU….will be able to see those bigots, haters, judgmental people die! Won't you be so happy then! You will have a title and a kingdom of your own! Please go to all the meetings you can to get the Kundalini spirit! This spirit will give you what you were looking for. It's better than that other spirit that is too restrictive with all those boundaries!

This spirit will give YOU bliss and Christ-consciousness! It will be a snake crawling up your spine to touch your Chakras, but it will be great in the end! YOU will be walking around like Zombies looking like you're high all the time saying, "wooah-man", etc. You'll love it!

Also…please bring your African drums and all your mystical romantic music because it will attract the people by the millions! Yes…bring that New Age music! We love romanticism with these spirits! Don't you love the delicious fruit on this tree?

Yes…YOU will build a great kingdom here because when YOU partner with THE COMMUNITY; YOU will travel, have money, and have all YOU want here.

YOU will be very blessed here because remember, we're the ones dallying out words declaring blessings and money is coming all the time. Remember, you can even sell your prophecies in your own kingdom! You are about to have all your heart's desires in this kingdom; worldly-wise that is. You will have the accolades of men, a title, belong to the "community", and a part of the universe.

The god on the inside of you will arise in this great Christ-consciousness! YOU will discover that YOU are just as much a part of this new "kingdom" and very much needed. Thank YOU for joining THE ONE WORLD RELIGION. PLEASE EXTEND YOUR HAND SO THAT WE MAY MARK IT WITH 666.

DISCLAIMER Halfway through the Tribulation, the Antichrist is going to destroy you, but it's OK while it lasts...right? You're building your KINGDOM NOW!

Clash of Two Kingdoms

In the very near future this will be evident. It will be a modern-day showdown between false and real prophets. Will the real prophets please stand up? The true prophets will continue to expose them and reveal the truth. Many in the church are deceived in this hour and believe they're in the right kingdom. We must pray they see the light.

CLASH OF TWO KINGDOMS

Bible Says "Judge by the Fruits"

Kingdom Now

Church is Christ/
Little gods

Experience over Word

Contemplative Prayer

KUNDALINI SPIRIT

7 Mountain Mandate – take over the world

Prideful

NAR extra-biblical

Follow teaching

after signs

FALSE UNITY/ ECUMENICAL

Mix w/ New Age & Occult

Dominionism

One World Government & Religion

Peace ahead & Utopia (Bliss)

We are the Bride
Ministries

Kingdom Come

Word is Foundation

Antichrist is Coming on the Scene

Judgment
Coming

Truth

Mark of the Beast is coming

Persecution

Martyrdom

True Holy Spirit

Preparing the Bride

Protects Christians

KN - Tree of Knowledge of Good & Evil
KC - Tree of Life
wearethebride.us

Which kingdom are you in?

8

United Nations Agenda 2030

The United Nations (UN) is a global network of countries in unison for a global agenda to take over the world. They formed in 1945 and formed Israel. Is that as much shock to you as it was to me? Yes, they did. However, before I get into all that, let me explain what the United Nations is about. According to their website, www.un.org, it explains:

Overview

The United Nations is an international organization founded in 1945. It is currently made up of 193 Member States. The mission and work of the United Nations are guided by the purposes and principles contained in its founding Charter.

Member States

Each of the 193 Member States of the United Nations is a member of the General Assembly.

States are admitted to membership in the UN by a decision of the General Assembly upon the recommendation of the Security Council.

Main Organs

The main organs of the UN are the General Assembly, the Security Council, the Economic and Social Council, the Trusteeship Council, the International Court of Justice, and the UN Secretariat. All were established in 1945 when the UN was founded. (United Nations, 2020)

Official Purpose of the United Nations

On the UN Facebook page they state;

Mission

Every day the UN works to tackle global challenges and deliver results for those most in need.

Giving life-saving support to populations hit by humanitarian crises, helping build and keep the peace in conflict-ridden areas, supporting governments and their citizens to advance development and fight poverty, and promoting human rights worldwide are the core pillars of the work of the United Nations and the mandates it receives from its Member States.

The Charter of the United Nations is available in full at http://www.un.org/en/documents/charter/. (United Nations, 2020)

Odd Things About UN

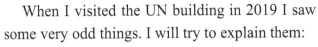

When I visited the UN building in 2019 I saw some very odd things. I will try to explain them:

Trump Tower is across the street facing the UN. I looked at that building and knew it could not be an accident. That is strategic.

Also, when you investigate Trump, you discover his dad's history of owning most of Manhattan and his ties to Orthodox Jews. I'll talk more about this later.

It's located right on the river. This represents transportation (water, etc.). There is a scripture right outside the UN. At first I thought that was great until I read Jonathan Cahn's book and realized it is a plant for the new world order agenda.

Listen at this unique perspective, "The United Nations takes the last part of verse 4 to tell Americans that God wants us to disarm. The UN ignores the part of Isaiah 2:4 about God being the "judge among the nations and shall rebuke many people." Isaiah 2:1-4 is in the future when the Lord will rule and reign from Jerusalem. The UN leaves out this part because the UN is made up of atheists that do not believe in the God of the Bible. The United Nations are hypocrites that use a Bible verse to disarm the American people and the world while not believing in the God who wrote the Bible verse." (King James Bible Study of Tulsa, 2017)

"Outside the U.N. building in New York there is a wall bearing the inscription, 'They will beat their swords into plowshares and their spears into pruning hooks. Nation will not take up sword against nation, nor will they learn war anymore. Isaiah.' But this is only the second part of the scripture verse, (Isaiah 2 v4)

'He will judge between the nations and will settle disputes for many peoples. They will beat their swords into plowshares and their spears into pruning hooks.' Nation will not take up sword against nation, nor will they train for war anymore."

This quotation out of context demonstrates the presumption of the nations, united in belief that they can bring in the peace of the Messianic Age, while not acknowledging God, whose word they are using." (Wild Olive, 2018)

In Jonathan Cahn's book, he uses that same scripture to announce unity among all nations and the messiah coming to Jerusalem. His narrative in that book plays right along with the New World Order agenda. This book is called *The Oracle*.

The UN's main heart is the sustainable developmental goals (SDG's). There are 17. They hope to achieve all 17 by 2030 with no man left behind. Of course they mean everyone that is antichrist. They do not want to partner with Christians. Their whole agenda is to annihilate us extremists.

This picture is when I visited the UN – September 2019.

The Sustainable Development Goals are:

1. No Poverty
2. Zero Hunger
3. Good Health and Well-being
4. Quality Education
5. Gender Equality
6. Clean Water and Sanitation
7. Affordable and Clean Energy
8. Decent Work and Economic Growth
9. Industry, Innovation, and Infrastructure
10. Reducing Inequality
11. Sustainable Cities and Communities
12. Responsible Consumption and Production
13. Climate Action
14. Life Below Water
15. Life On Land
16. Peace, Justice, and Strong Institutions
17. Partnerships for the Goals

By Unknown - un.org, Public Domain,
https://commons.wikimedia.org/w/index.php?curid=80531292

SDG's & Mark of the Beast Technology

Through these goals, the United Nations will be moving forward with their goal of taking over the world and implementing the one world order. What I mean by one world order is all of the nations under one government. It is one body ruling all nations.

This is what the Bible warns us about.

As part of the SDG's for Sierra Leone, they are implementing the first digital ID economy through blockchain technology. This technology is just another word for storing your data (information) in the cloud.

Your bank accounts, etc., will no longer be in a physical building. It will all be digital.

The United Nations is using this country as its first guinea pig. It appears that poor Africa is being used to practice for the beast.

Here is how they describe it;

At the Seventy-third Session of the UN General Assembly last year in New York, the President announced a partnership with the UN and KIVA, a US-based financial services international nonprofit organisation, to launch a bold new initiative designed to give the country's seven million citizens access to financial services.

"*Today, less than one year after, I am pleased to announce that we have accomplished that objective. My Government has developed a National Digital Identity Platform (NDIP). I am informed, and I announce with pride, that this is Africa's first Blockchain and Decentralised National Digital Identity System*", he said, *adding that the advent would radically change Sierra Leone's financial inclusion landscape and make it possible to access and deliver economic and other opportunities to every citizen.* (Daramy, 2019)

"The goal is, 'to provide all citizens of Sierra Leone with the ability to own and use their national civil identity – digitally,' according to Kiva. 'With just a thumbprint and their national identification number, Sierra Leoneans will in the years going forward be able to open or access an account at any financial institution in the country'." (Corum, 2019)

Not too long ago they did something like this in India where they have a national ID system as well. In America by October 2020 we are required to have Real-ID if we want to go in public governmental buildings or fly in planes.

It is a phase before the digital ID. They are setup with scanners, etc., ready for your hand to scan across it.

Here is that information:

The Department of Homeland Security (DHS) announced on December 20, 2013 a phased enforcement plan for the REAL ID Act (the Act), as passed by Congress, that will implement the Act in a measured, fair, and responsible way.

Secure driver's licenses and identification documents are a vital component of our national security framework. The REAL ID Act, passed by Congress in 2005, enacted the 9/11 Commission's recommendation that the Federal Government "set standards for the issuance of sources of identification, such as driver's licenses." The Act established minimum security standards for license issuance and production and prohibits Federal agencies from accepting for certain purposes driver's licenses and identification cards from states not meeting the Act's minimum standards.

The purposes covered by the Act are: accessing Federal facilities, entering nuclear power plants, and, no sooner than 2016, boarding federally regulated commercial aircraft.

DHS is committed to enforcing the REAL ID Act in accordance with the phased enforcement schedule and regulatory timeframes and is not inclined to grant additional extensions to any states that are not both committed to achieving full compliance and making substantial and documented progress in satisfying any unmet requirements. It has been 12 years since the REAL ID Act was passed and half of all the states have already met the REAL ID minimum standards. It is time that the remaining jurisdictions turn their commitments to secure identification into action. (DHS, 2020)

Also on that website look how they describe what the Real ID is, "The REAL ID Act establishes minimum security standards for license issuance and production and prohibits Federal agencies from accepting for certain purposes driver's licenses and identification cards from states not meeting the Act's minimum standards. The purposes covered by the Act are: accessing Federal facilities, entering nuclear power plants, and, boarding federally regulated commercial aircraft" (DHS, 2020).

When I went to New York last year for the United Nations General Assembly, I was at the train station and they had the weirdest device. I had to go LIVE and show everyone! It is a scanning machine ready for the chip!

The United Nations 17 SDG's is to monitor and prepare for the one world order in each nation. This year (2020) they began the UN Decade Action which means they are accelerating their agenda. Read more at https://unsdg.un.org/2030-agenda/decade-action.

Spiritual Warfare & Agenda 2030

There are several spirits behind this agenda. First is Leviathan – He is the chief demon of pride. He is a twisting demon. He twists things and perverts them. He lies to people and ends up twisting around them like a big fat snake and chokes the spirit out of them. It drains them dry. Many people don't realize this, but when you get tattoos, you are inviting that spirit in. Therefore, when people get tattoos they get obsessed with SELF. This is big in the NAR movement (New Apostolic Reformation), as this group really promotes the love of self and power. You will see as we explore it in this book. Many of their leaders are loaded with tattoos. This is one of the indicators of the Spirit of Leviathan.

We all know about the Jezebel spirit. This is a controlling spirit. This is definitely what the UN wants – to control the masses.

The Kundalini Spirit is a false holy spirit. It's not the true one. It brings euphoria and bliss and a false "love". It mocks the Holy Spirit. It is like a snake as well. When you "awaken" the Kundalini spirit, it is like a snake running up your spine and activates all of your chakras. Then when you receive your blissful state, it opens your third eye. This is the goal of many New Agers. Many people in the glory stream receive this spirit and you can tell. They walk around saying "wooah", jerk, hiss, see numbers all around them, etc. They also have a constant state of bliss to where they look goofy. This spirit is also very selfish. It cannot get enough of it. It's like it is searching for the next high.

The Cain Spirit is a murderous prideful spirit. It works in unison with Leviathan and Jezebel. Think of Cain and Abel. They were brothers. One got jealous because of how God saw their gift and killed the other. This is what is happening now with this apostasy.

As the false evangelicals partner with the Beast, they will eventually kill the true Christians. It will be just like in Jesus' day. We will be killed by our own people.

They all work together in this false unity movement and great deception. Be aware, sober and alert Bride.

This Leviathan, Jezebel and Cain spirit have all taken over our government and the church. They are squeezing the church into submission. It all partners with the UN Agenda 2030 vision. By 2030 they want all humans chipped (RFID). They know that the only thing holding them back from accomplishing that mission is the evangelical church. So, what did they do with President Trump?

They partnered with him, brought the enemy in (us) to the White House and gave us access to power. Then the church became even more drunk with power.

Two and a half years into his presidency he tests the church for loyalty (will explain later) then he goes after the LGBTQ and colors. (Democratic party). He is drunken for power and wants all.

It's funny that when Kanye West met him at the White House in

2018, he Tweeted and said they are both dragons. I never forgot that. A year later Kanye is traveling promoting a false Jesus and the church is falling right in. **They are all working together! Republicans & Democrats! You will learn in these books they want all types of people so they just push their propaganda where they can understand it.**

America, UN & Agenda 2030

According to this American LGBTQI group, UNAUSA, we pay the UN $1.81 per person to fund the USA's role in the UN. Look:

The average American pays just $1.86 each year in taxes to cover our country's regular budget dues to the UN. (UNAUSA, 2019)

Did President-elect Donald Trump declare we will pull out of the UN? However, we've been very engaged over the past three years since he's been in office. Why?

"Most people suppose that the U.N. is the world arbiter on all matters of right and wrong between nations; it certainly claims to be. But in whose name and on whose authority does the United Nations act and make its pronouncements?

It was not appointed by God, but by governments - in the human model of democracy and voting in proportion to representation. As such it is a human or humanistic organisation, placing human decision making as its highest criterion. Therefore, the Christian should not accept without question, the wisdom of such a world system, whether it be the U.N. or some other." (King James Bible Study of Tulsa, 2017)

When President Trump ran for office he promised to get out of the UN. He knew exactly how to pull in the evangelicals. Why? Because he had Paula to guide him.

The church would not be aboard his team if they knew what he is doing now. What if we would have known back in 2016 that he would be at the UN every year (now three years) and be giving them millions of dollars? We would certainly be hesitant because we associate the UN with globalist, New World Order and just plain evil. Now, three years later not only do we have the President STILL in there, but now we have all of the evangelicals that surround him are with him AT the UN! They are partnering with the other religions, LGBTQ and the UN under the name of religious freedom and social justice.

We cannot touch the unclean thing. We cannot partner with the UN no matter what! It is the Tower of Babel.

The evangelicals that have surrounded him have stabbed the church in the back and lie to them on weekly/monthly faith calls. They call in to the White House monthly and receive reports. Then the White House turns around and asks them to speak favorably on social media – or support the President on social media, etc.

America is so deep into the UN that we are on the board with Israel to push the LGBTQ agenda!

Only a few nations are on this board and we are one of them! This is why there is not a hesitancy to back away from the LGBTQ movement (WalkAway is a great example).

When you research Agenda 2030 milemarkers by the United

States you cannot find the reports, but you can on other countries. The US and UK reports are hidden to the US people. Other countries may be able to see it, but not us. Why is that? Maybe I'm not looking in the right place but I cannot find it. I suspect we are top on the list.

We house the UN. We recently banned a person from another country entering our country to address the UN. I would say that is a lot of power!

Davos – World Economic Forum & The Beast

In January 2020, he is speaking at Davos 2020. This is a global economic forum based upon the UN standards of Agenda2030. He is with them 100%. However, he promised during his 2016 election campaign that he was going to go after the globalists, back out of the UN and be a nationalist only. However, he is not. He is globalist all the way. Yes he does work to help our country come up, but he's doing it for Agenda2030. He is actually a speaker at the Davos 2020 event. They are working to improve climate change (an agenda of UN and one world order) and to improve more sustainability (UN term). Look at this from www.weforum.org/agenda/global

This Davos2020 is the World Economic Forum. They will be a huge part of the mark of the beast. They talk about human chip implantation (RFID chip) on their website, "The human body is the next big platform. The connected body is already a phenomena. And this implant is just a part of it. [...]We are updating our bodies with technology on a large scale already with wearables.

But all of the wearables we wear today will be implantable in five to 10 years. Who wants to carry a clumsy smartphone or smartwatch when you can have it in your fingernail? I think that is the direction where it is heading." (Ma, 2018)

They have many articles about technology control, surveillance, etc. They will probably be the brain of the beast. It is no coincidence that our President is speaking there.

UN & LGBTI

America is a member state of the UN LGBTI CORE GROUP. (UN LGBTI Core Group, 2020) There are less than ten nations in this group. Israel is in this group as well. Let's checkout their speech in 2019 at

74th SESSION OF THE GENERAL ASSEMBLY THIRD COMMITTEE

Agenda item 70 Promotion and protection
of human rights:

The UN Core LGBTI Group strongly believes that an inclusive society allows each person, including LGBTI people, to enjoy protection from violence and discrimination, as well as access to Human Rights.

To achieve inclusive societies and effectively implement the cross-cutting principle of the 2030 Agenda of Leaving No One Behind, a progressive realization of social, cultural and economic rights is essential, and therefore, we welcome the Report of the Independent Expert.

As the Secretary General said, "Hate speech is often used to dehumanize already marginalized groups and individuals, exacerbating discrimination and inciting violence. It is an attack on the very essence of Human Rights and affects us all. Hatred against the LGBTI community is perpetrated by people of all types, including religious and political leaders, and is amplified through traditional and social media. Very often there is no real protection. Conversely; in many places LGBTI people face being prosecuted and punished for their sexual orientation or gender identity."

We take this opportunity to express our support and pay tribute to human rights defenders working for the human rights of LGBTI people and others committed to combat violence based on sexual orientation, gender equality, gender expression and intersexual status Their work, which is often carried out with considerable personal risk, plays a critical role in denouncing human rights violations and abuses, providing support to victims, and sensitizing governments and public opinion. Through his work,

We are fully committed to addressing these violations and abuses - at national, regional and global levels, including through concerted and constructive participation in the United Nations. And while we seek support from all Member States for this cause, we would like to emphasize that opposing violence and discrimination is not and should never be the subject of controversy. It is fair and human.

Thank you. (UN LGBTI Core Group, 2019)

On their website this is their mission:

Principle 1

Raising awareness about LGBTI issues;

Principle 2

Contributing to multilateral work and negotiations at the United Nations, and;

Principle 3

Seeking common ground and engaging in a spirit of open, respectful and constructive dialogue and cooperation with UN Member States and other stakeholders outside the Core Group.

Core Group History

Background

The United Nations LGBTI Core Group is an informal cross regional group of United Nations Member States established in 2008. The group is co-chaired by Argentina and The Netherlands, and includes Albania, Australia, Bolivia, Brazil, Cabo Verde, Canada, Chile, Colombia, Costa Rica, Croatia, Ecuador, El Salvador, France, Germany, Israel, Italy, Japan, Luxembourg, Mexico, Montenegro, New Zealand, Norway, Spain, Sweden, the United Kingdom of Great Britain and Northern Ireland, the United States of America, Uruguay, the European Union (as an observer), as well as the Office of the UN High Commissioner for Human Rights, and the non-governmental organizations Human Rights Watch and OutRight Action International (Secretariat).

Goal

The overarching goal of the UN LGBTI Core Group in New York is to work within the United Nations framework on ensuring universal respect for the human rights and fundamental freedoms for all, specifically lesbian, gay bisexual, transgender and intersex (LGBTI) persons, with a particular focus on protection from violence and discrimination.

Can you believe we are in this group as one of the MEMBER STATES? Can you believe we help the UN to promote these values across the world? What about Israel? Well, it is shocking to find out that Tel Aviv is the highest population of LGBTQ!

Here is a recent event:

On 17 May, the UN #LGBTI Core Group will host a special event for International Day Against Homophobia, Biphobia and Transphobia to celebrate allies.

Picture from https://www.facebook.com/events/EUatUN/un-lgbti-core-group-event/430095587411798/

It is a shame that our government partners with this agenda, yet we have evangelicals in the White House attempting to convince Americans that we are on the greatest cusp for revival. God cannot bless a country that shoves vomit all over the world. It reminds me of the Great Whore/Babylon spoken of in Revelation.

WE WILL ANSWER TO GOD FOR THIS

UN FREE & EQUAL in USA

In New York we have this:

THE UNITED NATIONS' GLOBAL CAMPAIGN AGAINST HOMOPHOBIA AND TRANSPHOBIA

WHY?

More than a third of the world's countries criminalize consensual, loving same-sex relationships, entrenching prejudice and putting millions of people at risk of blackmail, arrest and imprisonment. Many countries force transgender people to undergo medical treatment, sterilization or meet other onerous preconditions before they can obtain legal recognition of their gender identity. Intersex children are often subjected to unnecessary surgery, causing physical and psychological pain and suffering. In many cases, a lack of adequate legal protections combined with hostile public attitudes leads to widespread discrimination against lesbian, gay, bisexual, transgender and intersex people – including workers being fired from jobs, students bullied and expelled from schools, and patients denied essential healthcare.

WHAT?

In July 2013, the Office of the United Nations High Commissioner for Human Rights (OHCHR) launched UN Free & Equal – an unprecedented global UN public information campaign aimed at promoting equal rights and fair treatment of LGBTI people. In 2017, UN Free & Equal reached 2.4 billion social media feeds around the world and generated a stream of widely shared materials – including powerful videos, impactful graphics and plain-language fact sheets. Several campaign videos – including a popular Bollywood-themed clip "The Welcome" – rank among the most watched videos ever produced by the United Nations. National UN Free & Equal campaigns and events have been organized in almost 30 countries, with visible support from UN, political, community and religious leaders and from celebrities in all regions of the world.

WHO?

The UN Free & Equal campaign is an initiative of the United Nations Human Rights Office and implemented with support from UN and non-UN partners at the country level. A number of celebrities have been named as campaign "Equality Champions" – including U.S. singer Ricky Martin, South African musician Yvonne Chaka Chaka, Bollywood actress Celina Jaitly, Brazilian pop star Daniela Mercury and her wife Malu Verçosa Mercury, U.S. hip-hop duo Macklemore and Ryan Lewis, and the band fun. Other prominent supporters – many of whom have taken part in campaign events – include South African Archbishop Emeritus Desmond Tutu, tennis legend Martina Navratilova, U.S. basketball champion Jason Collins, Indian actor Imran Khan, U.S. actor Zachary Quinto, and musicians Melissa Etheridge, Sara Bareilles and Rachel Platten. (UN Free and Equal, 2020)

Quote from the Secretary General

"I appeal to all governments and societies ... to build a world where no one has to be afraid because of their sexual orientation or gender identity."

UN Secretary-General António Guterres

What Does This Mean to Us?

This means huge trouble is on the horizon.

This is a plot with the UN to take the Christians out. This will lead to the great persecution coming very soon Bride.

This matters to you because they are pushing an agenda to form the one world order by 2030. They are controlling the masses through media, education, law enforcement, religion, etc. This matters because you need to know the strategy of the enemy.

They are all working together Bride. The government is not your friend. They are working with the Beast. We must prepare our families and obey God in the streets. It's all about souls. Never forget that.

9

Noahide Laws & Orthodox Jews

I did not know about the Agenda 2030 until I moved to Washington DC. I certainly did not know the connection between the Orthodox Jews, Noahide Laws and the UN. I knew that President Trump's son-in-law – Jared Kushner was an Orthodox Jew and that Ivanka had converted to Judaism when they got married. I fully saw the impact of this agenda when I visited the United Nations in September 2019. The sustainable developmental goals (SDG's) for the Agenda 2030 are all over the building. They are very serious in their intent to take over the world with the one world order.

There is a movement in the UN – led by the United States – to bring all faiths together. It is so sad to say but the United States is partnering with the POPE to usher this in. They are calling it **The Abrahamic Faith Initiative.**

Their manual - *The Peace Booklet* describes it as:

The purpose of this lesson is to introduce the learners to the notion that faith communities establish norms for their parishioners as well as for people outside the faith community.

In Judaism, this occurred through the Noahide laws. The texts included in this lesson will focus on the development of the Noahide Laws and the implications of creating standards for those "outside" the community. It is hoped that the learners will recognize that even though an individual may be of another faith, he or she can still be respected as a human being, because he or she may have in common some of the universal values that are shared by the Abrahamic faiths. (Abrahamic Faiths Peacemaking, 2012)

In this manual it provides a map for leaders to work together. In the forefront is the goal of the Noahide Laws. This is how they are pulling everyone together. Let's just go to our roots. Let's go back to where we was all in unity before Abraham.

According to the Ambassador of the US at the Holy See;

The Gregorian University is a place where you, as faith leaders, can consider the important questions raised by Pope Francis at the Global Conference of Human Fraternity in Abu Dhabi.

It was here that the Holy Father asked:

"How do we look after each other? "How do we nourish a fraternity which is not theoretical, but translates into authentic fraternity?" And "how can religions be channels of fraternity, rather than barriers of separation?"

The answers to these questions are fundamental to achieving real and lasting peace and understanding between the Abrahamic Faiths.

As President Trump said in Riyadh during his first presidential overseas visit, "If these three faiths can join together in cooperation, then peace in this world is possible.

The Abrahamic Faiths Initiative, in short, is predicated and built upon a message of hope." (U.S. Embassy to the Holy See, 2020)

Abrahamic Faith Peace Initiative

https://abrahamicfaithspeacemaking.com/

ABRAHAMIC FAITHS COVENANT FOR PEACEMAKING

As Jewish, Christian and Muslim people we find common ground in our common origin. We are followers of Abraham, committed to the human family and therefore adhere to a common core of ethical standards. We shall pursue friendship, peace and justice. We will speak out against all forms of prejudice, hatred, and discrimination.

We shall stand for the religious pluralism and mutual understanding that undergird the resilience of America.

As people of faith we enter into sacred covenant with a pledge to:

1. Pursue courageous friendships that bridge cultural divides.

2. Weave our lives and institutions into the fabric of safety and security, protecting all from intimidation, threats or war within community and country.

3. Speak and participate in public life, guided by prayer, reflection and experience. We bring our faithfulness to the public square to preserve religious pluralism, engendering peace in the 21st Century.

4. Shun passivity for creative and responsible imagination for the future and wellbeing of all people.

May these humble efforts be transformative in a world that cries out for peace and dignity.

We need to know this Bride because our Secretary of State's office is the one's behind this. The International Religious Freedom office is the catalyst for all this false unity.

Institute of Noahide Code

As you examine their Facebook page it proclaims, "The Laws of Noah: Peace, Unity and love for all, to teach how we can all live together perfectly by following the Universal Noahide Code UNC." (Cohen Y. D., 2020).

They are pushing the UN to bring unity to the world through these laws. They have been working on this for a very long time. They deceive the masses by making them think that it's biblical from back in Noah's day, but it is not. It is mixed with Kabballah and mysticism.

However, according to the Institute of Noahide Code - www.noahide.org, the Seven Laws are as follows:

Know G-d
Knowledge of the One True G-d
Respect G-d
Respect G-d's Holy Name
Respect Life
Respect the Sanctity of Human Life
Respect Marriage
Respect the Traditional Family
Respect Property
Respect the Property of Others
Respect Animals
Respect All Creatures
Preserve Justice
Establish a Righteous Judicial System

A robust and healthy legal system, administering justice fairly, creates a society worthy of G-d's blessings. Establishing a system of judges, courts, and officials to maintain and enforce the law is a far-reaching responsibility.

This precept translates the ideals of our personal life into a formal order for society at large. It is the extension and guarantee of all the preceding laws. (Institute of Noahide Code, 2020)

This organization has a petition on www.change.org and it states, "What is most beautiful about these laws, is the breathing room they provide. They resonate equally in Africa, (North) America, (South) America, Antarctica, Asia, Australia and Europe.

They are like the guidelines of a great master of music or art: firm, reliable and comprehensive -- but only a base, and upon this base each people and every person may build.

The Universal Noahide Laws are a sacred inheritance to all humanity, that every person on the face of the earth can use as the basis of his or her life. If enough of us will begin to incorporate these laws into our lives, we will see a different world very soon.

The Institute of Noahide Code INC – United Nations-accredited NGO (ECOSOC) - headed by Rabbi Yaakov David Cohen, aims to promote peace, democracy and harmony in the world through the values represented by the seven laws of the Universal Noahide code UN. (Cohen Y. D., 2020)

Noahide Laws and the United Nations

This is how they describe it to the world, "Our world is plagued by wars, famine, natural disasters, and violence. The United Nations was created as a platform for all the nations to get together and help promote peace and prosperity for all of humanity. But so far we can see that even a tiny change takes years to agree upon.

215

The time has come for the people to nudge the UN in the right direction.

Wouldn't It be Easier if We All Spoke the Same Language???

The team at Noahide.org believes that if all the nations had a common language, a common set of principles, it would unite all the world's leaders and help bring world peace faster.

It is time that we bring back the Universal Noahide Code, which helped establish judicial systems around the world hundreds of years ago. (Cohen Y. D., 2020)

They have been working the United Nations to implement these laws for years now and have made a lot of leeway. Now with the newly-formed Abrahamic Peace Initiative sponsored by our very own Secretary of State's Office, we are in it head-first. How sad is this? This is what they desire – one of their events (the ecumenical movement – one world religion).

One God Day
International Center for Ethno-Religious Mediation

All religions in the world observe holy days in addition to one day every week that each religion devotes to prayer.

ONE GOD DAY

One God Day is an international observance day to encounter people of other religions, faiths or beliefs in order to increase mutual respect, understanding, empathy and

We believe there should be a special day in a year designated for an international observance of the One God who is worshiped or revered in all religions, faiths, beliefs, mystical groups, sciences, and so on. On that very day, the world should pause and remember the Supreme Being each group holds in high reverence.

An international acknowledgement or recognition of the Supreme Being worshiped by all religions, faiths and beliefs in the world through the observance of One God Day will serve as the basis for interfaith or inter-religious dialogue and also help to promote religious freedom in countries around the world. Most importantly, it will help to prevent and reduce religiously motivated violence - such as violent extremism, hate crime, and terrorism - thereby strengthening international peace and security.

One God Day is an initiative of the International Center for Ethno-Religious Mediation, a New York based 501 (c) (3) nonprofit organization in Special Consultative Status with the United Nations Economic and Social Council (ECOSOC). (ICER Mediation, 2019)

Check this out at a college: "Three Abrahamic congregations in Omaha, Nebraska, have created the Tri-Faith Initiative, building separate houses of worship and a shared community center to promote peace and understanding among communities of different faiths." (Faith & Leadership, 2018)

Bride, this is growing at a very fast pace. It's very sad that our own evangelical leaders are partnering with all this mess.

Press Release 01/14/2020 from State Department about Ambassador of Religious Freedom traveling to Vatican City:

Ambassador Brownback will begin his trip in Rome and Vatican City, January 14-16, where he will participate in the launch of the <u>Abrahamic Faiths Initiative</u>, a dialogue led and organized by religious leaders of three Abrahamic faith traditions, Judaism, Christianity, and Islam, working together to emphasize the peaceful expression of faith and the renunciation of violence.

This dialogue, the first of many, seeks to foster mutual respect, tolerance, and understanding between the Abrahamic faith traditions in the quest for greater religious freedom, stability and peace around the world.

Final Warning about Noahide Laws

The United Nations created the State of Israel (they call them states). You can research it. The Zionists (Rockefellers, globalists, and so happens to be the prosperity – glory-faith teachers too) are partnering with the Vatican and Orthodox Jews to form the one world religion and government. They are setting the stage for the Antichrist to step on the scene.

This is what they're doing by distracting you with all the fighting in Washington DC. All of that is fake, a facade! Do not believe it. What they are doing behind closed doors is very dangerous. The tech companies are moving at warp speed to get blockchain in motion – the new global currency and microchip.

The Noahide Institute is working side by side with the United Nations to implement this when the time is right. Sounds like they've made it all the way to our White House and Secretary of State.

What this means to you church is that this is how they're going to kill you. By President Trump signing all these executive orders about anti-Semitism is lining it up for the court tribunals, death squads, etc. When you study the Noahide.org website you will see that they believe in death by decapitation. They do not want anyone saying to the Jews that they must convert to Christianity and accept Jesus into their heart. If you believe that Jesus is the only way to Heaven you will die.

Why? Because they are merging all religions into ONE (As One) because they believe that all gods are the same and if you try to say that your God is better than their god then you will be killed. You will be a fundamentalist, hater, anti-Semite, terrorist, bigot, fascist, etc. For sure you will be an extremist. They want to rid the world of all extremist in all religions.

When President Trump passed the law of prayer in schools many Christians think that it is a huge victory. It's not. It is a setup for those Noahide Laws to begin the old ritualistic prayers in schools. Watch what I'm saying.

By the mainstream Christian media stations pushing the Messianic Judaism the past few years and the old Hebraic ways, they are lining up with this agenda. People don't know it but they are just priming their hearts to accept the "roots" of the Bible. When they tell the world to go back to the Old Testament and do away with the New Testament, many Christians will go along with this Noahide Laws. They will gladly accept this because their big leaders will push them down this path. Do not do it Bride. Hold your ground.

Also, many of those ministry leaders are 501©3 organizations and they are setup with the Department of Homeland Security. Did you know that?

They are instructed as they receive money from the government to cooperate with them in the state of emergencies and turn their people in to the government. In other words, they will partner with them and not you. Look at this from Department of Homeland Security:

Identified Outcomes from Engaging Faith-based and Community Organizations Emergency managers using this engagement approach uncovered previously unknown assets within local faith-based and community organizations. Faith-based and Community Organizations can:

♣ Serve as communication hubs to distribute trusted messages

♣ Host Community Emergency Response Team (CERT) classes and other trainings

♣ Be used as points of distribution for emergency commodities and supplies

♣ Provide staging area and reception sites for emergency services

♣ Support mobile feeding and transportation services

♣ Provide housing assistance and other social services

♣ Join a Voluntary Organizations Active in Disaster (VOAD) network Members of these organizations can:

♣ Provide psychological first aid

♣ Provide emotional and spiritual care

♣ Help conduct welfare checks in the community (DHS, 2018)

When you consider these same churches are teaching pre-trib rapture so that when the mark of the beast comes you will take the mark.

Their argument is that it cannot happen until Jesus takes us all home so you can go ahead and take the CHIP. Also the church is in la-la land because they feel like they do not have to prepare and fight because Jesus will rescue them and they will not suffer. Isn't it also funny that these same type of churches do not preach about suffering, persecution (except because you're blessed and others are jealous), less of you and more of Jesus, repentance, etc. The pre-trib rapture has robbed the church greatly and it cannot be backed up in scripture. The Holy Spirit had to teach me because that doctrine was engrained in me.

What is wrong with going through Tribulation? See the pre-trib teaches they will not have to suffer and go through any of Tribulation. Well, we will. In my *The American Judgment* book, we will talk about future scenarios to consider. I consider myself a Harvest-Trib person. Lord I can do anything with you so take me as far as I can go to win souls and to help the Kingdom of God! We can do it all because he is with us.

Then we also have a President now who has partnered with the evangelical church and presenting a picture to the Bride that is false. This is to pull your enemies in closer. We will talk more about that next.

Dr. June Dawn Knight

10

President Trump &

The Evangelicals

This is the biggest question I receive since I left the White House. Is President Trump in the apostasy? The answer is yes. He is a part of the big picture, in spite of what they are trying to portray on social media and the propaganda through the media. He and Paula White have had this planned for a long time. Paula even said in an interview that she met with him in 2011 to plan for his presidency. She also said she's been friends with him over 17 years. All this time we thought God did a miracle and he won supernaturally, and it's not true. It is all planned. Back in the early 90s he was interviewed by Oprah and she asked him if he would consider running for president and he said "only when the country is ready and they need him." Now that I'm putting all this together I realize that the country had to fall with Obama, go through the terrible things we did in order for President Trump to come in and be our "savior".

By him including Paula White, it was to pull the enemy in closer. This is strategic to pull in the evangelicals, give them power, put them in the White House, invite them to meetings, have prayer meetings, etc., so that it looks like he's including us. It's strategic.

I can hear many of you screaming at me about how wrong I am in this assessment, and I totally understand. When I first went to the White House in 2018 I was fully a Trump supporter. I was all the way up until I went to the United Nations in September 2019 and saw the apostasy on full display. It was my last straw with him. I saw the apostasy and I do not want to be a part of the propaganda and lies. The church has been duped. We've been misled. We still are!

Ecumenical Partnership w/Evangelicals

A lot of the things that President Trump does that makes the Christians feel like he's doing so much for us is mixed with other religions. It's not just for Christianity, it's for ALL FAITHS. The Christians do not realize the serious implications of what he is doing.

One example is the recent change to allow prayer back in elementary schools and allows high schools to treat religious organizations the same as other organizations. On the face of this it sounds like a dream come true. However, picture this. What if Muslims take over a school, or witches, satanism or even LGBTQ (which is trying to become a religion). By President Trump not specifically pointing out Christianity, he's opening the door for your teachers to indoctrinate, etc. Look at this:

Additionally, the guidance describes the Equal Access Act requirements. The Equal Access Act applies only to public secondary schools or public high schools, and it requires that religious student groups receive the same access to facilities such as classrooms as secular student groups.

So if a religious student group would like to hold a prayer meeting in the classroom, that religious student group may do so as long as a secular student group can reserve that same room for a secular activity. (Office of the Press Secretary, 2020)

They are so careful to not show the evangelicals the ecumenical partnerships. Either that or they have Paula there to make it look like that the evangelicals are OK with this action the President has taken. For instance, when they showed the video of the President signing the paper it had all different religions behind him hid. It did not show a woman with a hijab on behind him etc. At least it didn't on this White House video:

https://www.facebook.com/WhiteHouse/videos/3933122613380742/

Everything his administration does for the faith community is not only for Christianity. I hope you know that. At the National Day of Prayer it is an ecumenical event. They have people from all faiths praying.

He has had Muslim events at the White House and all other events. He is not only evangelical-pleasers.

As One Movement

Paula White began this prayer call initiative when she took over in the White House. What they do not tell you all is that on the phone with you evangelicals is all the other faiths. She was at the UN with all the other faiths pushing religious freedom, which is all ecumenical. She has become the ecumenical queen while in the White House, with the face of an evangelical. It is a false agenda. It is a facade. Almost all faith initiatives announced with the President are with all the other religions too so why would you think this initiative is any different church? It's not.

225

Donald Trump and Martyrdom

I have a theory. I am watching as all this unfolds, but I want to submit it to you Bride so that your eyes will be open and watching.

I remember when President-elect Donald J. Trump was on CBN television a few days before his election. At that time we had no idea who would win.

Donald was pleading to the church that he needs at least 80% of the Christians to vote for him or he will not win. Him and his wife both pled with the Christians to vote for him.

He pledged his loyalty to our causes and would support us, etc. Then the miracle happened. When he was announced as the winner EVERYONE was shocked! Well without making this too long because I will go into this in more depth in *The Last American Bride* book; I believe that the world knew that the evangelicals are the ones that put him in. Instant anger towards us arose from the left.

We all saw how they showed out acting like a bunch of cry-babies. So, since then the left has been trying their hardest to crack this shell. They want us to drop DJT because they know we are his solid rock.

This was all pre-planned however with Paula White. Years ago, back in 2007, she did an interview where she talked about her divorce (On Larry King Live) and they talked about the support from President Trump. She even moved in Trump Towers after the divorce for years. This has been a coordinated effort to be the final stage of the one world order and the only way they could do it is to have the evangelicals on board.

So, the left is very angry about this new merger (or so they're making us think this) and one of their attacks is on our data on social media. It is all a setup.

They tapped into all the evangelical's data so that they can try to expose us and crack us from the inside out. Exposure is coming as part of our judgment. The Lord's already spoken this to me. So, keep your eye out Bride.

Oh, the main point I was making that each day the mainstream media continues to bridge this divide us against the world. How terrible we are and hypocrites because we support that man.

This thing they're doing with white supremacy, etc., is all together. They're trying to say that Christianity is a white man's religion as well.

They want to build up more anger at the fundamentalist evangelical Christians…which will eventually lead to our demise.

When the exposure comes, Facebook has already cleaned their hands since Zuckerberg went to the Senate and now they can just blame it on Cambridge Analytical. Pretty slick I think. Keep your eyes open!

Pulpit and Pen website explains a lot of what is going on behind closed doors to shift our nation left through the church and they explain, "It is no secret that evangelical America is the last remaining demographic standing between the preservation of American culture and globalist progressivism. If that demographic could be changed or swayed, then the victory of the American left – and by vicarious accomplishment, international globalism – would all be assured." (NEWS DIVISION, 2018)

Bride, you really need to read this article they wrote because it explains how the global elites met in Washington DC in May 2018 to discuss how to turn the evangelicals to the left!

They are trying to spin the church completely around to this new world order and one world church.

I also want you to pay attention to how the left (people who are liberal and worldly) are getting so angry at the Trump supporters. Why? Because they cannot understand how the church can support such an evil man (in their eyes).

So, due to his pride and arrogance, they feel like this reflects on the church. What they do not realize is that God is using his pride and arrogance to accomplish his mission. Who else could stand up to the beast?

Atlantic Magazine (a liberal magazine) states, "'The Church is in one of its deepest moments of crisis—not because of some election result or not, but because of what has been exposed to be the poverty of the American Church in its capacity to be able to see and love and serve and engage in ways in which we simply fail to do. And that vocation is the vocation that must be recovered and must be made real in tangible action.' There are countless examples of how such tangible action can be manifest. But as a starting point, evangelical Christians should acknowledge the profound damage that's being done to their movement by its braided political relationship—its love affair, to bring us back to the words of Ralph Reed—with a president who is an ethical and moral wreck. Until that is undone—until followers of Jesus are once again willing to speak truth to power rather than act like court pastors—the crisis in American Christianity will only deepen, its public testimony only dim, its effort to be a healing agent in a broken world only weaken. At this point, I can't help but wonder whether that really matters to many of Donald Trump's besotted evangelical supporters." (Wehner, 2019)

We sit back in awe of how he can stand up to all the attacks daily. We assumed it is because the church is praying a wall of fire around him. However, it appears that he is working with the UN, globalists and new world order agenda. Why do I say that? I saw it because of what I saw in DC and the evidence. In this book I do not have enough space to give very specific details to all the areas I speak of. However, I hope to begin teaching and revealing the specifics.

One example I can explain now is this article:

Evangelical Christians are now backing an actual pimp in a Nevada election

Dennis Hof owns five brothels, but all conservative Christians care about is that he's a Republican.

https://www.lgbtqnation.com/2018/06/evangelical-christians-now-backing-actual-pimp-nevada-election/

This is written from the LGBTQ Agenda website:

But just when you think the hypocrisy has gone as far as it possible can, along comes Dennis Hof.

Hof, 71, is seeking a seat as a Republican in the Nevada state legislature. He styles himself "the Trump of Pahrump," the town in which resides.

Hof also happens to be a pimp. He owns five brothels, including the Moonlite Bunny Ranch, and a strip club. His sex empire that has made him a wealthy man. He's appeared on an HBO reality series and even written a book about it: The Art of the Pimp.

A man who made his fortune as an actual peddler of flesh should give Christian voters pause. In Hof's case, not so much. Instead, evangelicals lined up to vote for him and engaged in mental acrobatics to justify their support.

In their mind we have lost it. We support a President who makes fun of people all the time on Twitter, calls people names, makes fun of poor people, and who has no couth. They feel like we are such hypocrites. Not only that but look how we now partner with the Walk Away movement supporting LGBTQ agenda. They think we are hypocritical for that too. We ARE!

Basically the non-Christians are looking at a church who has watered down the gospel to partner with other religions and LGBTQ to support a man in office. We have compromised God's word and God's face to be seen with the powerful. Is it worth it church? This is what we need to ask ourself. Is all this worth it in the end? We will stand before a holy God about touching all these other idols for an end-mean.

So, Here's My Theory in a Nutshell

I believe President Trump is being used by the globalist to incite anger against the church. The more he Tweet's the mean and crazy things the angrier the left becomes to us. As we defend his mean behaviors (non-Christian attitudes), then we are reflected as a bunch of hypocrits. We are seen as double-minded people. We allow this President to say god-d*** at a public rally in July 2019 and say nothing about it! We allow to say the GD word TWICE and there's no repercussions from the evangelicals!

How crazy is this? So, my theory is that this is being done on purpose. President Trump is not dumb. He knows exactly what he is doing. I believe that when the time comes for them to come after the extremists (not the ones who have compromised the gospel), they will feel like they're doing God a favor by killing the goofy people. We sold our soul listening to our leaders who have partnered and agreed with perversion of the gospel, pride, bad behavior and other sins because we thought we needed someone in like that to tackle the Beast. But, guess what we got? We got the church that now endorses Kanye and the WORLD LOVES HIM TOO! We have Kanye at all these evangelical churches luring people to his Satanic old music and clothing that is still on his YouTube and online. The church is looking more like the pride and self-centeredness.

My theory is that it is all on purpose to take us down later. Pay attention Bride.

International Religious Freedom

The division from the U.S. State Department is called the International Religious Freedom. This is a catalyst for the one world religion. It is pulling all the religions together for "religious freedom and belief." However, they don't tell the church about BELIEF. Why? Because IT'S LGBTQ! They're blending them ALL.

Let's examine how they say it on their website:

As Secretary Pompeo stated in Brussels in December, the United States is dedicated to building a liberal order that supports "institutions that work in American interests" and in the "service of our shared values" with allies and partners around the world.

The Ministerial for Religious Freedom represents the kind of flexible, voluntary, and nimble multilateralism that serves nation-states' interests best.

The Ministerial and related events bring together an incredibly diverse group of religious leaders, government officials, civil society representatives, and people of faith for the common good. (State.gov, 2020). Notice the word "common good".

Here is their official mission:

The Ministerial reaffirmed international commitments to promote religious freedom for all and focus on concrete outcomes that produce durable, positive change. A broad range of stakeholders convened to discuss challenges, identify concrete ways to combat religious persecution and discrimination, and ensure greater respect for freedom of religion or belief. (State.gov, 2020)

Notice how they add the AND BELIEF. Let's examine what that means:

USAID and New World Order

USAID has partnered with the IRF and President Trump's Center for Faith and Opportunity Initiatives. This is led by Paula White. She is in the mix of all the mixing perversion.

This is their mission with the Faith Dept:

Working closely with faith-based and community stakeholders is critical to the success of USAID's mission. These efforts are coordinated through USAID's Center for Faith and Opportunity Initiatives (CFOI).

We provide a bridge for faith-based and community groups seeking to connect with USAID's mission by directing them to appropriate points-of-contact within the Agency, offering resources to help guide them through the partnership process, and providing information about new grant opportunities.

We convene faith-based and community groups to catalyze new opportunities for collaboration between these groups, and between these groups and the government.

We help to eliminate barriers encountered by faith-based and community organizations seeking to partner with USAID on a range of global development issues including global health, child survival, and food security. (US AID, 2019)

US AID works alongside the State Department to define extremism. This is critical to us for the future. Here is their definition:

> **Countering Violent Extremism** refers to proactive actions to counter efforts by violent extremists to radicalize, recruit, and mobilize followers to violence and to address specific factors that facilitate violent extremist recruitment and radicalization to violence. CVE encompasses policy and activities to increase peaceful options for political, economic and social engagement available to communities and local governments and their ability to act on them.
>
> *Department of State & USAID Joint Strategy on Countering Violent Extremism*

The current director of this division (CFOI) graduated from her master's degree from a university in Rome. It's a Catholic university. Check out some of her experience:

Previously, Ms. Evans represented the United States Conference of Catholic Bishops in its ongoing relationship with national Muslim, Jewish, Sikh, Orthodox and Christian communities, including joint service collaborations, public policy analysis and advocacy, and inter-religious theological dialogue.

Ms. Evans holds a Masters degree from the Johns Hopkins School of Advanced International Studies (SAIS), with a focus on the role of religious actors in global affairs and development. She also holds a Masters degree in Religious Sciences from the Regina Apostolorum Pontifical University in Rome, Italy, and a specialization in International Human Rights Law from the University of Oxford. (US AID, 2019)

What they're really doing

The powers-that-be are preparing for the one world order. The image is that we are all so blessed because we have a President working so hard for us and fighting for religious freedom. It is all propaganda. I hope you see this by now.

Stephen Coughlin is an attorney and ex-FBI agent. He spoke at a conference in Virginia in 2019 and explained that the word "freedom" was built up by the Muslims. They actually use this term to destroy the Christian west. He also said, "You are supposed to lay down your life for your sheep. What's the point of being a shepherd if you don't know the wolf and where he is? The Bible says to feed my sheep, not feed my sheep to the wolves. He who is a hireling doesn't care."

You can watch this video at https://youtu.be/3Kgnv8enkg0. It is on the WATB.tv channel. He talks a lot about the Interfaith Movement.

He explains that when they use the bridge word to dialogue means to bring you over to their side. This video is a must because he busts out the darkness.

President Trump and LGBTQ

When he ran for office he did not seek help from the LGBTQ, only the evangelicals. So, when I moved to Washington DC and saw the WalkAway rally at the National Mall, the President of the group threatened the Republicans and the President. He said that they will partner with them for the 2018 elections, but if they do not turn towards LGBTQ agenda, they will leave in 2020. So, a week later the Lord gave me a dream and instructed me to address this to the President in public at the White House. This was so hard! When I arrived on a beautiful Saturday (the Saturday before elections – Nov 3, 2018), it looked like there were 300 people there from all over the world. I told the Lord he would have to hide me because I can't do this on my own. I had my speech written down. I setup my table in front of the back public side of the White House, pulled out my megaphone, and setup my live-streaming and began the speech. Here it is:

Excerpts from the Speech:

Yes, let me clarify that we are still facing judgment from God - it has already been written that it WILL HAPPEN.

However, We are the Bride Ministries is praying today that President Trump will either watch this video or God will put it on his heart to do a public repentance to God on behalf of this whole nation because that is the ONLY thing that will grant us more time! President Trump is put in a very special position right now. God has surrounded him with praying ministers and Godly council and I'm sure they are saying the same thing. OUR NATION MUST ADMIT ITS WRONG DOINGS TO GOD. WE MUST REPENT FROM OUR PRESIDENT DOWN or judgment will come sooner than later.

This is one reason I'm here. I'm to cry out to the President to consider God and allow God to fulfill his vision for America! God has a destiny for her and the church and we want to go out of here a victorious Bride. There will come a time when judgment will come but by then we hope that we have done all we can do to win the harvest. Our country WILL answer to God for the transgressions and errors! We must repent as a nation!

Later in the speech................................

Notice in this picture the man where the light is shining on. He was the mocker. I felt like God was shining his warning on him.

Continuing....................................

To the Republican Party:

I know there was much struggle when President Trump became the nominee. The established party rejected him and you know all the reasons, however, I want to applaud you for accepting him and rolling with God. This is why the evangelical church votes with you most every time. (The ones who vote according to their morals and not other agendas - vote biblically). We applaud you for keeping the Christian principals over the year such as:

• Pro-Life - we must protect the unborn! We must not dishonor God and keep this legal! We must tear down Roe vs. Wade!

We must repent to God on behalf of this innocence murder in our country! This is one thing we need to repent for ASAP!

• Anti-Gay Agenda - we must protect the institute of the righteous marriage in God's eyes which is between man and woman. There is no other gender. Let me say it again - there is no other gender. We are what we are born with and designed by God - not what was chosen at a fertility clinic, etc. God makes the choice and we declare today that marriage holy before God is between a man and a woman. Also we declare that God does NOT recognize marriage between same sex. That is an abomination in God's eyes and a stench in his nostrils. I pray today Republican Party that you will not back off your position on this because the church must not agree with the homosexual agenda. We must stick to the Biblical definition of marriage. In our eyes, the red that you have represents closest to the Biblical definitions like the blood of Jesus. Vote red - vote the blood on our nation! So, please Republicans keep the biblical position on marriage even if the #WalkAway movement is threatening you.

I heard their leader say the other day in DC that the Republican Party better pay attention because they are all leaving the Democratic Party and voting Republican THIS TIME and you better not forget it. He basically threatened that if you don't bend your position on the LGBTQ community that they will leave you too in 2020. Well let me stress to you Republican leadership that the church as a whole prays that you DO NOT BEND TO THEIR AGENDA AND HOLD YOUR POSITIONS. They are coming to us BECAUSE we are the party of peace! We are the party that is not violent and crazy. So, we believe it's because of the Christian agenda and heart of the Republican Party that gives this peaceful atmosphere.

So, please hold strongly to the Anti-Gay positions.

• Israel - The church respects your positions on protecting Israel - unlike the Democrats. Please hold your position and do not move away from it. God says we will be a blessed nation as long as we bless Israel and Jerusalem! **To President Trump - I ask you and beg you sir to NOT participate in the actions to require Palestine and Israel to give up land and sign a peace agreement for seven years. We Christians recognize that as an illegal action against God that will bring severe consequences to our nation.** We have had many prophecies that when this happens God will literally split our nation in half! We split Israel AND HE WILL SPLIT OURS! Hear me sir - God is not playing around - please do not do that deal! I realize you may be a part of organizing it but please do not coordinate that final move sir! The nation will pay a heavy price and time will be no more! It will officially kick off Tribulation! There is so much work God has for us to do before that hits so please do not do it! Work with the Christians to help our nation be restored to God and to grant us more time. I tell you sir -- it all rests on your shoulders. We pray you make the right decision when it comes to Israel. I don't know what other ministers are telling you about Israel, but I'm telling you that we cannot split Israel!

• To the Republican Party - I once again applaud you all for your hard work and persecution you've been through to side with the God agenda in our nation. We literally see it like that - Republicans represent good and Democrats represent evil. We believe that our nation is split but God is separating the wheat from the tares - good from evil. See the true Christians are not allowed to touch unclean things**. We are not allowed to partner with Satanic organizations, etc.** We must keep our separate identity unto God. This is why we cannot partner with the Democratic Agenda.

They have been taken over the demonic forces from Hell and their fruits are proof of it! So, please - keep the good and guard the gates. *I do want to say that I applaud the #WalkAway movement for all they've done and leading people to the Republican Party - but I do want to say that just because you came to the right does not mean that you can hold them hostage either. You know what you're getting into so I pray you can adapt and understand the reasons why they have their certain agendas.*

• Let me clarify that just because we do not support the Gay agenda does not mean we do not love the people. Of course every one is an American from all backgrounds. It doesn't matter if you're gay, transgender, white, black, brown or red, we are ALL Americans. I'm strictly talking political positions and agendas. If an organization leans right due to biblical values, then we cannot back off of that and we will still love you anyway inspite of our differences. It's the same with Christianity - we love the person, just not the sin and we can separate the two. We cannot participate in the

241

sin, but we can certainly reside in the same country, etc. Our country is GREAT because God made it Great! We have all this greatness BECAUSE OF GOD! We as Christians merely back up his word and cannot back off of it. God is holy and thus he cannot partner with unnatural things and unholy things. God wants all humans to be set free from perversion and wickedness. The devil is the one who wants to pervert identities and change people from who God really called them to be! So, yes we can all exist together in our country but we cannot change our laws to permit perversions or wickedness. We must defend the institution of the family and nation. We will not apologize for God's position on sin.

We can lead you to the cross so that God can heal the individual and they can become all that God has called them to be. God has better!

Later on........................

There's one last area sir that MUST be dealt with from your level in order to achieve your heart's desire and that is REPENTANCE TO GOD for the sin's and transgressions of our country to Him. See, God has brought me here to confirm to you sir that this IS God's request to you to SEAL THE ULTIMATE DEAL OF ALL TIME!

You think Israel is the biggest deal of the Century....sir...that is NOT. The biggest deal of the Century is to please God before He takes you home. You will leave a legacy that even Heaven will applaud if you will HONOR HIM AND REPENT ON BEHALF OF THIS COUNTRY FROM things that former presidents have done that have brought shame on this country such as Obama and the Supreme Court passing laws such as gay marriage, abortion, etc. God's desire for you sir is to REPENT and say it out of YOUR MOUTH that you officially recognize the transgressions of our country and you repent FROM YOUR OFFICE. God wants to open up the windows of Heaven to this country so that we can fulfill our destiny BEFORE He comes and brings the FINAL JUDGMENT. I'm telling you sir...judgment will happen because it's been written, but God wants to give you this final DEAL OFFER - which is to partner with Heaven and bring true health to the country SPIRITUALLY.

THIS IS WHY GOD BROUGHT ME TO WASHINGTON DC is to deliver this message to you sir.

I finished that one as I was greatly persecuted by the LGBTQ man screaming the whole time. Praise God! When I gave that speech I had no idea that just six months later he would take a downturn and spiral towards the LGBTQ.

Right before I left DC, God had me address him again in front of the White House. This was a final warning from God. I did a Trump March called Evangelicals for Trump. I planned this before I discovered that he has other intentions than we thought for evangelicals. I wanted to cancel so bad but God wouldn't let me. Then, right before the march he gave me a warning speech for the President and nation.

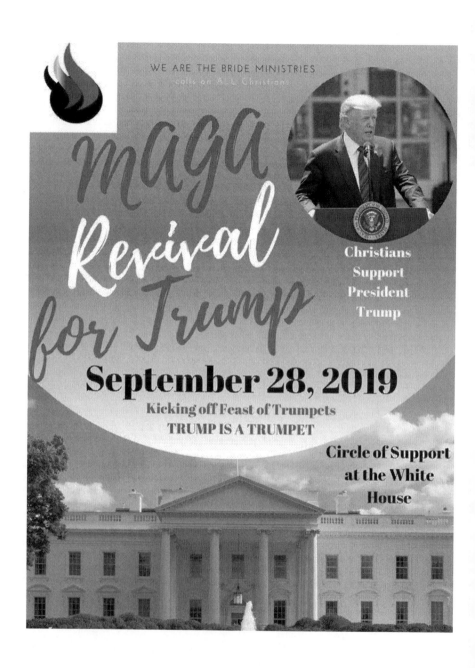

Americans, I stand here today and I am honored to be in front of the greatest house in the land. The White House!

This house is white and I believe it represents purity of our country and God's heart towards her. It is also an honor that my ministry is called We are the Bride and it represents the pure Bride. When I say Bride I am referring to the Body of Christ, the people who are born again. These people have given their life to their savior, Jesus Christ. He died on the cross for their sins and became a dowry to God for his Bride. This makes this Body of Christ the actual Bride of Christ. We are looking for that blessed day of Jesus coming in the clouds to take us home. Yes we do believe it will be a supernatural experience.

One day the church will disappear and appear with her husband in Heaven and we will celebrate together the marriage supper of the Lamb. Yes, we may disagree on when this may happen, pre-trib, mid-trib or post-trib, but as long as we know he IS returning. The preterist who believe he came in 70ad - we reject that theology. We believe he IS coming back soon! So, now you know why I say "Bride" - it means to the church as a whole across the world. They are my target audience. This is the evangelicals.

Bride, I stand here today on this Saturday, September 28, 2019 to declare that we ARE a Christian Nation! We still believe this and we will fight for her! God gave this land to the Christians just as he did many other peoples in history such as Joshua with Jericho or Abraham with other lands. God gave the Christians this American land. Yes, we were not perfect in how we took the land, but we desired to have a land where we could worship our Lord without persecution and without the State running it. We escaped the British country so that we can truly worship and serve our creator.

Today we stand here as Americans, rich and poor, of every tribe and tongue and we all love our Lord Jesus Christ.

Today is a testimony of Jesus. All the lives represented here has a story to tell. OUR STORY IS FOR GOD'S GLORY! This march is not just about our President Donald J. Trump and his victory in 2020…but it is about YOU…EVERY CITIZEN! EVERY PERSON! The Democrats have stolen our identity and the FAKE NEWS MEDIA! They have told you that our country IS NOT GREAT. People…our country CAN ONLY BE GREAT IF GOD IS AT THE HEAD! Many judgments have come because people left GOD out. We actually had a president in the White House last term who told OTHER COUNTRIES that we are NOT a Christian nation! He denied God and forcefully PUSHED HIM OUT. We now have a President who brought him back in! He has prayer meetings all the time, asks for people to pray, brings them to the platform to share stories, etc. HE HAS SAID MANY TIMES, "WE DO NOT WORSHIP GOVERNMENT – WE WORSHIP GOD." Through this President we have brought God back in. No, he is not perfect…but are you? NO! None of us are perfect. Yes, we pray for him and his mouth. We see it too. However…we believe that as he fights for the swamp to be drained and for law and order to come back to our country, that he sometimes gets on the level as the Democrats. We do not need to get on their level because they are godless to begin with. We do not endorse the Democratic party because they partner with everything anti-God – antichrist. God would never support the LGBTQ agenda, same-sex marriage, or abortion. Much less how they treat Israel.

So, the Democrats have stolen the identity of the country. HOWEVER TODAY…WE ARE HERE TO SAY THAT WE ARE TAKING IT BACK!

YOU CANNOT HIJACK OUR COUNTRY ANY LONGER! THIS COUNTRY BELONGS TO GOD AND FOR HIS PURPOSE! OUR GOD IS HOLY! By them taking God out of the Legislative Branch they have spoken and released a curse over themselves. LET GOD HAVE JUSTICE TODAY. WE DECLARE JUSTICE! God must be returned AND OUR NATION MUST REPENT!

WE CARE MORE ABOUT GOD'S FACE AND IMAGE THAN WE DO OUR AGENDAS! We must repent for taking him out! He is holy!

The Democrats have also tried to imply to man that MAGA is terrible and that it WAS NEVER GREAT. Let me inform them of something. American people are very real people and they each have amazing stories of struggle, triumph and dreams. ONE OF THE MAIN REASONS OF AMERICA BEING SO GREAT IS BECAUSE WITH GOD AT THE HEAD, WE CAN TRULY DREAM! We are in a country of capitalist. This means that we can become anything we want to be! I am a great example of that because I was born in a poor family, etc. However…at age 41 I went back to college and went for seven more years all the way to achieve my Doctor! I was able to change my whole identity! If it was up to the Democrats, we would be a socialist nation and I wouldn't be able to be GREAT.

YOU ARE GREAT AMERICA! YOU ARE! YOU ARE WHAT MAKES AMERICA GREAT! NOT WHITE SUPREMACY LIKE THE DEMOCRATS TELL YOU…BUT YOU AS A HUMAN. God has opened up a land that you can flower and bud so beautifully if you work hard enough. He has truly blessed this land inspite of our treating him terribly.

Inspite of us spitting in his face…HE HAS STILL HAD MERCY AND GRACE TOWARDS US!

You are what makes America great! Let me encourage you today America…DREAM AGAIN! DREAM! WHAT HAS GOD CALLED YOU TO DO? DON'T LET THE DEMOCRATS HOLD YOU BACK…OR THE FAKE NEWS MEDIA! BELIEVE GOD! NOT THEM!

Remember too America that God has brought us through many trying times…many battles…AND WE COME THROUGH THEM ALL! God does have a timeclock…we know time will end ONE DAY..however…God chose you to live FOR SUCH A TIME AS THIS. THIS IS YOUR NATION. THIS IS YOUR TIME. ARE YOU GOING TO LET IT GO TO THE ENEMY OR ARE YOU GOING TO STAND UP AND FIGHT AND TAKE YOUR COUNTRY BACK WITH GOD AS THE HEAD!!!!!

WHO IS KING OF THIS NATION?

WHO IS GOD OF THIS NATION?

WHO MAKES AMERICA GREAT?

WHO MAKES YOU GREAT?

So…I'm encouraging you today to allow yourself to DREAM AGAIN. Allow yourself to take pride in your country. This is YOUR COUNTRY. OWN IT. Don't let the crazy left steal your joy and pride of the greatest country in the world!

To the Republican Party & To President Trump:

This has to do with the #Trump2020 campaign. Please do not partner with the LGBTQ agenda. Yes, we love all people…but we are not to endorse that community and partner with it. The Evangelical church voted you in and we will KEEP YOU IN. We care more bout God's face and favor towards us than man's. We do not want judgment to hit our country YET SIR. Please do not do this. God has a plan and we want to achieve that goal.

Please hear the sound of the glory of the Lord today. God loves America and has a plan for her. He wants to use her and we must REPENT AS A NATION FROM THE PRESIDENT DOWN and allow God to truly replenish her!

Also President Trump…we need to repent to you because we have laid low and allowed you to take big hits. PLEASE FORGIVE US. We will step forward more and help you sir…just PLEASE DON'T PARTNER WITH LGBTQ agenda. Keep our nation clean before God. We care about his opinion on our nation. WE ARE A CHRISTIAN NATION.

Dr. June Knight
We are the Bride Ministries

I finished that speech and God called me out of Washington DC a couple of weeks later! He pulled me out! Now I see that the Beast is being setup at a very rapid speed and is not slowing down at all. The President is a genius! He has someone from every marketing demographic to be his voice to their specific people. Blacks, Latinos, LGBTQ, evangelicals, Islam, etc. I just pray that the true Bride will see through this One World agenda. I love you Bride.

Look at it like this. Trump has partnered with the far right in our country – NAR. Netanyahu has partnered with his far right – Orthodox Jews. So, look what they did. The mainstream Christian media is now infiltrated with Messianic Jews luring the Bride into the Hebrew Roots movement, Torah, Kabballah, numerology, mysticism, etc. They are pulling the church towards the Jews and away from Jesus.

When the Noahide Laws are implemented many Christians will already be there and happily denounce Christ. They are being lulled into a deep coma.

They call it Anti-Semitism to say that a Jew must be converted to Christianity and accept Jesus as their savior. Yet, this is what is required! Everyone – Jew or Greek, Jew or Gentile, man or woman must get saved. The enemy has crept in the church and our Christian media has partnered with this agenda.

On top of all this, our President signed an Executive Order to protect against Anti-Semitism! Why didn't he write one to protect the evangelicals? Wake up church. His father even gave enormous amounts of money to Chabad church in New York back in the 1950s. His family have roots in this. Be wise. "Mr. Fred Trump donated the plot of land where the synagogue was built and contributed towards the construction. He then attended the dinner every year and generously donated to the Beach Haven Jewish Center. He affectionately referred to Rabbi Wagner as "My Rabbi" at their yearly meetings." (Beach Haven Jewish Center, 2020)

Final Analysis

President Trump has been chosen years ago to be President now. This is all pre-planned, along with the support of the fake evangelicals. They are propped up to have the millions of supporters and now they can lure them towards this Antichrist coming. This group knows exactly what they are doing. We must be wise Bride. The mark of the beast is about to be rolled out along with the Tribulation period. Who knows what is coming next.

Dr. June Dawn Knight

11

Q&A and PRAYER

What is the Apostasy?

• The apostasy is the false religion that is working their plan to take over the world in a One World Religion. This will setup for the Antichrist about to step on the scene. This is the Catholic Church taking over all the religious systems in the world and causing all to worship the Beast. The Catholic Church is working alongside the Orthodox Jews to do the Noahide Laws and the UN. They're all together. The Bible talks about this coming.

How Do I Know if I'm in It?

• After learning what it is, the question to ask yourself is are you under this teaching? Are you in the NAR? EM? EC? If so, get out and renounce it! Many people are in this and are in it innocently. They do not even know this great plan is taking place. When they see these ministers, everything looks perfect. So, if you are in question, I encourage you to research it yourself (after you pray and ask Holy Spirit first). Search (minister's name) + (ecumenical movement) or (ecumenical) or (emergent).

Also, research who they are hanging around. This will tell you as well. Check out their websites and find out more about them.

Should I Talk to My Pastor About This?

• Yes, always talk to your spiritual parents. Tell them what you discovered. If you suspect they are in this, then pray about what to do. I do know this…you will be judged for staying under a false prophet.

What Do You Mean I'll Be Judged by Sitting Under False?

• I will talk more about this in *The American Judgment*. When God judges someone, he judges everything attached to it. The Bible says not to touch the unclean thing. God hates mixing.

What About Taking the Meat and Spitting Out the Bones?

• I've heard people say that. "I'll just listen to this music or preacher and spit out the bones of what I don't like." In the meantime, you're being infected with this virus.

What if it's in My House and Car?

• You need to get it out. You need to separate yourselves from the heresy. Throw the books, music, tapes, videos, booklets, and all away. Then pray to cleanse your house. This is serious business. He's coming back after a Bride without spot and wrinkle. Do you love them more than honoring God? More than holiness?

I Have Family Participating in This, What Do I Do?

• Try to talk to them if you can. Pray for them. Then, you need to examine your heart and ask God to deliver you from any part you played in it. Ask them to forgive you and ask God to forgive you. Pray and ask God to open their eyes too. Suggest these books.

How Big is This? How Many Ministries are Involved?

• You would be surprised to find out that it looks like most of the ministries are in this. Social media helped to spread it and open doors for them to all hook up and to invite friends to events, etc.

So, I'd say probably 80% of them. Almost every big-named preacher on TV is in it! It's sad and I'm sorry to report this.

Should You Be Mentioning Minister's Names & Ministries?

• Yes! The apostles called them by name. We must expose it. I agonized over this question for months. I sought much counsel. I know that most of them teach not to, but scripturally as a watchman on the wall, I'm required to. The Bible says to call out the false and to speak TRUTH. So, I must obey the Lord even if the world hates me. Jesus and the apostles did it! My book is designed to be bare-bones truth. When the Bride reads these books, they will have no question as to what it is so that they can be successful.

Why Are You Doing This?

• I'm doing this first because the Lord told me to. Secondly, it's because of the *MAGA Revival Tour* where God told me He was going to reveal the sickness in the church and it will bring great persecution, etc. He did.

I was sick about it. But, now I'm obeying Him and revealing it to the church in hopes that someone out there will seek God about it and get out! As I stated in the intro into the book, I am looking out for you and bringing all this research to you. Pray about it and ask the Holy Spirit what you are to do with the information and how can you be delivered from the apostasy, etc.

What Makes You Qualified to Write About All This?

• I asked God the same thing. Who am I? God replied, "You are my prophet. You are my servant." So, He did prepare me for such a time as this. I worked for a lawyer for a year in graduate school where I learned how to do research. God gave me an education and equipped me on how to search through the web, do web design, studying logos and graphic designs, advertisings, videos, etc. God basically trained me for this. I see so much! Most of all, He has called me to do this and anointed me.

I'm Scared About All of This. What Do I Do?

• Don't be afraid. God created you for such a time as this. God wrote about it and prepared us for it. Now it's been revealed, we must resist it and not take the mark!

How Do I Know if I Have the Kundalini Spirit?

• The Kundalini spirit is the false Jesus. It is an angel of light. You will know because of the symptoms I listed earlier. After your experience, did you have violent jerks in the middle of the night, or chaos suddenly appear in your life, sleepless nights, sexual demons visiting you, etc.

I Have Tattoos, How Can I Repent and Get Delivered? Same for All the Spirits You Talked About

• I suggest you find a deliverance minister. If you don't know one you can contact Restoration Church in Highlands Texas, Pastor Phillip Morris and there's many other ones. They can lead you in the right direction or answer your questions. You can also check out his website at www.drphillipmorris.org

Are We Close to The Great Tribulation & The Mark of the Beast? The End of Times?

• Yes, we are! I will discuss this more in The American Judgment.

Is it Necessary I Get the Idols Out of My Life Too? How Do I Know What They Are?

• First, an idol is anything that comes in between you and God. Anything that you cannot give up is an idol. For instance, if you're hurting inside about something and you go to relieve that pain somewhere else besides God, that is an idol to you. Some resort to eating, sex, drugs, rock and roll, fighting, drinking, yoga, relationships with other people, children, etc. Whatever you love more than God is an idol to you.

To find out more read the next book, *The American Idols*.

What is an Apostle and Prophet?

• The Bible says that an apostle is a sent one. Many people describe them as church builders. The word apostle is mentioned 80 times in the bible and the word prophet is mentioned 454 times. Prophets are the mouthpiece of God. They speak truth and declare the judgments from God.

• Deuteronomy 18:18 - I will raise them up a Prophet from among their brethren, like unto thee, and will put my words in his mouth; and he shall speak unto them all that I shall command him.

• Galatians 1:1 - Paul, an apostle, (not of men, neither by man, but by Jesus Christ, and God the Father, who raised him from the dead;)

How Do People Get Those Titles?

• Should be given by God and confirmed by others.

Why Should We Expose?

• Galatians 1:6-9 - 6 I marvel that ye are so soon removed from him that called you into the grace of Christ unto another gospel: 7 Which is not another; but there be some that trouble you and would pervert the gospel of Christ. 8 But though we, or an angel from heaven, preach any other gospel unto you than that which we have preached unto you, let him be accursed. 9 As we said before, so say I now again, if any man preaches any other gospel unto you than that ye have received, let him be accursed.

• Philippians 1:7 - Even as it is meet for me to think this of you all, because I have you in my heart; inasmuch as both in my bonds, and in the defense and confirmation of the gospel, ye all are partakers of my grace.

If President Trump is a part of the Globalist agenda & UN, what are we to do?

Do what we've always done. Vote for the lesser of two evils. If you vote, we always have to vote towards the conservative agenda.

Whether the vote counts or not only God knows, however, we will have done our civic duty before God to vote closer to our biblical values. Also, do not get caught up in the spirit of Democrat/Republican, black/white, etc. Don't get caught up in the "I'm the victim" syndrome of Trump. They are doing this to build loyalty. They are getting you to feel sorry for him so that you will defend him and they can fulfill their agenda. Get your house in order and do not be consumed with the antichrist agenda.

Prayer for Deliverance & Freedom

Dear Jesus,

Please help me to see the truth. I do not want to be blinded to the enemy right now. I recognize I'm in spiritual warfare and I want to be free from ungodly associations, attachments, allegiances, and the unclean thing. I do not love the world more than I love you Lord. Please set me free from ALL influences of this apostasy! Help me to have the courage to say no and not go with the crowd or flow to be accepted by the majority. Help me to have the courage to stand up for truth in this hour, even at the cost of my life. I love you more than I love my life. I love truth more than I love my reputation.

You died for me Jesus and now I'm choosing with my will to die for you to all that I hold precious in my life. I die to all my allegiances and loyalties, except to you. I pledge my allegiance to the King of Kings and Lord of Lords.

Please help my family to see the truth Lord and to not fall for the beast system. Please help me to have a love for the word more than ever. Teach me and show me the truth. In Jesus' name, Amen!

OK Bride. Now we will learn about the idols in the church in the next book, *The American Idols*. This is very important because the church and our individual lives will be judged based on these things and we need to be free! *The American Judgment* will help you to prepare. Then the last book is *The Last American Bride* in which I will talk to you about what is coming down the pike and how to be ready when it's your time to meet your destiny.

Apostasy + Idolatry = Judgment & it's for the Harvest

Thank you for reading this book.

Love you, Dr. June Knight, We are the Bride Ministries

References

Abrahamic Faiths Peacemaking. (2012, October). *For One Great Peace Study Guide*. Retrieved from Abrahamic Faith Peacemaking: http://abrahamicfaithspeacemaking.com/wp-content/uploads/2012/10/For-One-Great-Peace-Study-Guide.pdf

Addison, D. (2018). *Tattoo & Piercing Interpretation Course*. Retrieved from DougAddisom.com: https://dougaddison.store/product/tattoo-piercing-interpretation-course

ADF. (2018, May 16). *Court orders end to abortion-pill mandate for Oklahoma Christian universities*. Retrieved from Alliance Defending Freedom - ADF Legal: https://www.adflegal.org/detailspages/press-release-details/court-orders-end-to-abortion-pill-mandate-for-oklahoma-christian-universities

Apologetics Index. (2018, March 24). *Manifested Sons of God*. Retrieved from Apologetics Index: http://www.apologeticsindex.org/m22.html

Beach Haven Jewish Center. (2020, February 15). *About Us*. Retrieved from Beach Haven Jewish Center: https://www.beachhavenjc.org/about-us

Bell, R. (2016, May 01). *Rob Bell / Everything is Spiritual (2016 Tour Film)*. Retrieved from YouTube: https://youtu.be/JT09JbaEh_I

Berean Call. (2019, January 26). *THE SEND'S LOU ENGLE BLESSES THOSE HELPING THE "EVANGELICAL AND CATHOLIC WORLDS BECOME ONE"*. Retrieved from Berean Call: https://www.thebereancall.org/content/send-s-lou-engle-blesses-those-helping-evangelical-and-catholic-worlds-become-one

Bethel Church. (2018, January 08). *Christalignment*. Retrieved from
Bethel Church: http://www.bethel.com/about/christalignment/

Bethel Ministries. (2018, March 27). *Bethel School of Technology*.
Retrieved from Bethel Tech: https://betheltech.net/

Bickle, M. (2001, July 19). *Contemplative Prayer*. Retrieved from
mikebickle.org:
https://drive.google.com/drive/u/0/folders/1C4zDUpQ-
jR5nO6kuGUkjhIbzx4kk1Nj1

Bounds, E. (1984). *Guide to Spiritual Warfare*. New Kinsington, PA:
Whitaker House.

Britannica. (2018, April 08). *Mysticism*. Retrieved from Britannica
Encyclopedia: https://www.britannica.com/topic/mysticism

Cambridge. (2018, May 16). *Definitions*. Retrieved from Cambridge
Dictionary:
https://dictionary.cambridge.org/us/dictionary/english/recant

Carey, J. (2018, April 08). *Spiritual Life: The Emerging Church Explained*.
Retrieved from CBN: http://www1.cbn.com/spirituallife/the-
emerging-church-explained

CBN. (2018, April 06). *Baptism in the Holy Spirit*. Retrieved from CBN:
http://www1.cbn.com/spirituallife/what-is-baptism-in-the-holy-
spirit

Chadbourne, E. (2020, February 15). *Eddy Manson Biography*. Retrieved
from All Music: https://www.allmusic.com/artist/eddy-manson-
mn0001180245/biography

Christalignment. (2018, March 27). *Christalignment*. Retrieved from
Christalignment: http://www.christalignment.org/

Christians Together. (2011, February 17). *Kingdom Now teaching: beware*. Retrieved from Christians Together in the Highlands and Islands: https://www.christianstogether.net/Articles/244590/Christians _Together_in/Survival_Kit/Kingdom_Now_teaching.aspx

Church of Satan. (2020, January 15). *FAQ - Fundamental Beliefs*. Retrieved from Church of Satan: https://www.churchofsatan.com/faq-fundamental-beliefs/

Cohen, Y. D. (2020, January 06). *About*. Retrieved from Facebook.com: https://www.facebook.com/pg/Laws.Of.Noah/about/

Cohen, Y. D. (2020, September 06). *United Nations Universal Peace*. Retrieved from Change.org: https://www.change.org/p/united-nations-universal-peace

Cokesbury. (2020, January 20). *The Inclusive Bible*. Retrieved from Cokesbury: https://www.cokesbury.com/9781580512138-The-Inclusive-Bible

Cortes, A. (2017, September 12). *After-school Satan club tests the limits of church and state*. Retrieved from KALW Local Public Ratio: http://kalw.org/post/after-school-satan-club-tests-limits-church-and-state#stream/0

DeBruyn, L. (2014, August 29). *The Physics of Heaven: A Serial Book Review & Theological Interaction: Pt 1*. Retrieved from Herescope: http://herescope.blogspot.com/2014/08/the-physics-of-heaven.html?m=1

DHS. (2018, June). *Engaging Faith-based and Community Organizations*. Retrieved from Department of Homeland Security: https://www.fema.gov/media-library-data/1528736429875-8fa08bed9d957cdc324c2b7f6a92903b/Engaging_Faith-based_and_Community_Organizations.pdf

DHS. (2020, January 06). *Real ID*. Retrieved from Department of
Homeland Security: https://www.dhs.gov/real-id

Erdmann, M. (2013, December 21). *What Is Dominionism?* Retrieved
from Deception in the Church:
http://www.deceptioninthechurch.com/ditc47-2.html

Faith & Leadership. (2018, May 1). *Christians, Jews and Muslims share a
campus in a unique interfaith collaboration*. Retrieved from
Faith & Leadership: https://faithandleadership.com/christians-
jews-and-muslims-share-campus-unique-interfaith-
collaboration

Fisher, C. (2015, January 07). *Bethel Music; a Work of Darkness*.
Retrieved from Truth Keepers:
http://www.truthkeepers.com/?p=754

Foxe, J. (2018, March 22). *Fox's Book of Martyrs*. Retrieved from The
Project Gutenberg:
http://ihtys.narod.ru/foxes_book_of_martyrs.pdf

Garth, L. (2011). *The Naked Truth*. Revell.

George, T. (2008, September 08). *Protestants Can Affirm the
"Communion of Saints" and the "Holy Catholic Church."*.
Retrieved from Chriistianity Today:
https://www.christianitytoday.com/history/2008/september/w
hat-do-protestant-churches-mean-when-they-recite-i.html

Gowdy, P. (n.d.). *The Toronto Deception*. Retrieved from Deception in
the Church:
http://www.deceptioninthechurch.com/TheTorontoDeception.
htm

Graham, B. (1974). *Billy Graham Speech at 1st Congress*. Retrieved from Lausanne: https://www.lausanne.org/content/why-lausanne-print

Hamill, J. (2002, December 19). *PROPHETS POINT TO "THE CALL - KANSAS CITY"*. Retrieved from Elijah's List: http://www.elijahlist.com/words/display_word/1381

Hamill, J. (2018, April 10). *METRO Facebook can predict people's behaviour by spying through their smartphone, patent reveals.* Retrieved from Metro News.uk: http://metro.co.uk/2018/04/10/facebook-can-predict-peoples-behaviour-spying-smartphone-patent-reveals-7452861/

Herescope. (2007, July 09). *As in Heaven So on Earth*. Retrieved from Herescope: http://herescope.blogspot.com/2007/07/as-in-heaven-so-on-earth.html

Herrin, J. (2014, June 03). *Deception - Part 4*. Retrieved from Parables; Bringing Hidden Truths to Light: http://parablesblog.blogspot.com/2014/06/deception-part-4.html

Hilborn, D. (2000, December 14). *A CHRONICLE of the TORONTO BLESSING*. Retrieved from The Evangelical Alliance: http://www.banner.org.uk/media/books/A%20chronicle%20of%20the%20TB%20by%20David%20Hilborn.pdf

Hillsong. (2018, February 08). *The Alpha Conference*. Retrieved from AlphaUSA.org: https://alphausa.org/alpha-national/the-alpha-conference

ICAL. (2018, April 08). *Statement of Faith*. Retrieved from ICAL Leaders: https://www.icaleaders.com/about-ical/statement-of-faith

ICER Mediation. (2019). *One God Day*. Retrieved from ICER: https://www.icermediation.org/projects-campaigns/one-god-day/

ImageNet. (2016). *About ImageNet*. Retrieved from ImageNet: http://image-net.org/about-overview

Institute of Noahide Code. (2020, January 06). *Seven Laws*. Retrieved from Noahide: http://noahide.org/sevenlaws/

Jefferies, M. (2017, July 17). *Hillsong, Bethel Music and The Great Seduction*. Retrieved from Emergent Watch: https://emergentwatch.com/2017/07/17/hillsong-bethel-music-and-the-great-seduction/

Johnson, B. (2000, July 21). *Bill Johnson Quotes*. Retrieved from Bethel Music: https://bethelmusic.com/blog/bill-johnson-quotes/

Johnson, B. (2003, January 01). *When Heaven Invades Earth*. Retrieved from Google Books: https://play.google.com/store/books/details/Bill_Johnson_When_Heaven_Invades_Earth?id=msDOo0EM6ucC

Johnson, B. (2014, April 11). *Don't Worship the Bible - Bill Johnson*. Retrieved from YouTube: https://www.youtube.com/watch?time_continue=26&v=J5Bh5NMyhyA

Johnson, B. (2017, May 13). *A Mess- Heidi Baker - Bill Johnson - Rolland Baker - Bethel Redding*. Retrieved from YouTube: https://www.youtube.com/watch?v=vbEpJU1UMR0

Joyner, R. (2006, April 01). *"Taking the Land--The Coming Kingdom"*. Retrieved from Elijah List: http://www.elijahlist.com/words/display_word.html?ID=3948

Keckler, C. (1999). *From Convent to Pentecost*. Retrieved from Christian Hospitality: http://www.christianhospitality.org/resources/charlotte-convent-to-pentecost.pdf

King James Bible Study of Tulsa. (2017, March 19). *Isaiah Wall of the United Nations*. Retrieved from King James Bible Study of Tulsa: http://www.kingjamesbiblestudyoftulsa.com/king-james-bible-study-of-tulsa-blog/isaiah-wall-united-nations/

KOHLER, P. (2016, September 19). *What Is Kingdom Now Theology?* Retrieved from Salvation and Survival: https://www.salvationandsurvival.com/2016/09/what-is-kingdom-now-theology.html

Lausanne.org. (2018, April 08). *Our Legacy*. Retrieved from Lausanne Movement: https://www.lausanne.org/our-legacy

Mason, P. (2016, October 20). *Covert Operations - Ministry in the New Age*. Retrieved from PhilMason.org: http://philmason.org/2016/10/20/covert-operatives

Mason, P. (2016, October 20). *The Glory of Christ's Kingdom*. Retrieved from PhilMason.org: http://philmason.org/2016/10/20/the-glory-of-christs-kingdom/

Mattera, J. (2017, January 17). *Last Days Views That Lead To Semi-Gnosticism*. Retrieved from Joseph Mattera: http://josephmattera.org/last-days-views-that-lead-to-semi-gnosticism/

McCumber, M. (2012, August 26). *Taking Dominion- Do We Really Want God's Kingdom Now?* Retrieved from Deception Bytes: http://deceptionbytes.com/taking-dominion-do-we-really-want-gods-kingdom-now/

Mohoric, M. (2012). *Energy Healing ~ Alternative Medicine*. Retrieved from Gigong Energy Healing: http://www.qigongenergyhealing.com/

NAIOTH COLLEGE. (2017, August 21). *NAOITH College*. Retrieved from Facebook: https://www.facebook.com/tribebyronbay/photos/a.19695598 0468162/802205536609867/

NEWS DIVISION. (2018, March 27). *Charismatics Now Using "Christian" Tarot Cards*. Retrieved from Pulpit and Pen: http://pulpitandpen.org/2017/12/11/charismatics-now-using-christian-tarot-cards/

nl, B. f. (2018, March 27). *Monstrance*. Retrieved from Wiki Media: https://commons.wikimedia.org/wiki/File:Monstrans.jpg

Oakland, R. (2004). *Another Jesus? The eucharistic Christ and the New Evangelization*. Silverton, OR: Lighthouse Trails Publishing.

Oakland, R. (2007). *Faith Undone*. Eureka, Montana: Lighthouse Trails Publishing.

Oakland, R. (2012, May 26). *The Facts Behind My Departure from Calvary Chapel*. Retrieved from Lighthousetrailsresearch.com: https://www.lighthousetrailsresearch.com/blog/?p=9360

Odle, D. (1998). *Grace Abuse; One of the Greatest Hindrances to Genuine Revival*. Write Hand Publishing.

Odle, D. (2012). *The Polluted Church; From Rome to Kansas City*. Opelika, AL: BookBaby.

Office of the Press Secretary. (2020). *Background Press Call by Domestic Policy Council Director Joe Grogan and Senior Administration Officials on New Rules to Protect Religious Freedom.* Washington DC: White House.

Oliver, M. (1996, July 16). *Eddy Manson; Noted Harmonica Player.* Retrieved from LA T imes: http://articles.latimes.com/1996-07-16/news/mn-24749_1_harmonica-player

Pagitt, D. (2018, April 08). *A Christianity Worth Believing.* Retrieved from Doug Pagitt: http://www.dougpagitt.com/new-page-1

Rand, L. (2016, January 26). *New Communion Words.* Retrieved from TonyJones.net: http://tonyj.net/blog/2016/01/26/new-communion-words/#sthash.4B3ya7NM.dpbs

Reagan, D. D. (2018, April 28). *The One World Religion.* Retrieved from ChristinProphecy.com: http://christinprophecy.org/articles/the-one-world-religion/

Régimbal, F. J.-P. (2015, October 23). *Examples of Subliminal Messages in Rock Music.* Retrieved from Tradition in Action: http://www.traditioninaction.org/Cultural/D054_Rock_4.htm

Saavedra, R. (2018, June 24). *Maxine Waters Calls For Attacks On Members Of Trump Administration.* Retrieved from The Dailywire: https://www.dailywire.com/news/watch-maxine-waters-calls-attacks-members-trump-ryan-saavedra

Schrock, D. (2017, March 01). *Book Review: When Heaven Invades Earth, by Bill Johnson.* Retrieved from 9Marks: https://www.9marks.org/review/book-review-when-heaven-invades-earth-by-bill-johnson/

Spreeman, A. (2019). *Everything You (and your Pastor) Must Know About the NAR*. Retrieved from Berean Research: https://bereanresearch.org/everything-pastor-must-know-nar/

State.gov. (2020, January 11). *2019 Ministerial To Advance Religious Freedom*. Retrieved from State.gov: https://www.state.gov/2019-ministerial-to-advance-religious-freedom/

Strom, A. (2015, September 24). *BILL JOHNSON, BETHEL & the NEW AGE*. Retrieved from John the Baptist TV: http://www.johnthebaptisttv.com/

Suri, Y. (2014, September 24). *Gold Dust and Gems Falling From Heaven - Spiritual Adultery*. Retrieved from YouTube: https://www.youtube.com/watch?v=vb15EhgbvHA

TECC. (2018, April 18). *About*. Retrieved from Evangelical Covenant Church: https://covchurch.org/

Tennent, T. C. (2014, July 25). *Lausanne and Global Evangelicalism: Theological Distinctives and Missiological Impact*. Retrieved from Lausanne : https://www.lausanne.org/content/lausanne-and-global-evangelicalism-theological-distinctives-and-missiological-impact

TruNews. (2017, December 20). *Bethel Pastor Defends Use of Destiny Cards*. Retrieved from TruNews: https://www.trunews.com/article/update-bethel-pastor-defends-use-of-destiny-cards

TruNews. (2017, December 15). *California Megachurch Dabbling in Occult*. Retrieved from TruNews: https://www.trunews.com/article/california-megachurch-dabbling-in-occult

Truth in Reality. (2012, September 21). *What is Kingdom Theology and the Kingdom Now Teaching?* Retrieved from Truth in Reality: https://truthinreality.com/2012/09/21/what-is-kingdom-theology-and-the-kingdom-now-teaching/

U.S. Embassy to the Holy See. (2020, January 14). *Ambassador Gingrich's Remarks to the Abrahamic Faiths Initiative.* Retrieved from Vatican US Embassy: https://va.usembassy.gov/ambassador-gingrichs-remarks-to-the-abrahamic-faiths-initiative/

UN Free and Equal. (2020, January 10). *About.* Retrieved from UN Free and Equal: https://www.unfe.org/about/

UN LGBTI Core Group. (2019, October 18). *Intervention pronounced by Excma. Mrs. Egriselda Aracely González López.* Retrieved from UN LGBTI Core Group: https://unlgbticoregroup.org/2019/10/18/intervencion-pronunciada-excma-sra-egriselda-aracely-gonzalez-lopez/

UN LGBTI Core Group. (2020, January 10). *Members.* Retrieved from UN LGBTI Core Group: https://unlgbticoregroup.org/members/

UNAUSA. (2019). *Advocacy.* Retrieved from UNAUSA: https://unausa.org/advocacy/

United Nations. (2020, January 06). *About UN.* Retrieved from UN.org: https://www.un.org/en/about-un/

United Nations. (2020, January 06). *United Nations.* Retrieved from Facebook: https://www.facebook.com/pg/unitednations/about/

US AID. (2019, August 01). *Center for Faith and Opportunities Initiative.* Retrieved from US AID: https://www.usaid.gov/who-we-are/organization/independent-offices/cfoi

US AID. (2019, September 16). *Kirsten Evans*. Retrieved from US AID: https://www.usaid.gov/who-we-are/organization/kirsten-evans

Warren, R. (2020, February 15). *Rick Warren, Founder*. Retrieved from Pastors.com: http://pastors.com/about/

Wax, T. (2013, May 08). *John Stott Confronted Billy Graham*. Retrieved from The Gospel Coalition: https://www.thegospelcoalition.org/blogs/trevin-wax/when-john-stott-confronted-billy-graham/

WCC. (2005, October 21). *Ecumenical Movement in the 21st Century*. Retrieved from World Council of Churches: https://www.oikoumene.org/en/resources/documents/wcc-programmes/ecumenical-movement-in-the-21st-century/foundational-texts/the-future-of-ecumenism-in-the-21st-century

Wehner, P. (2019, July 5). *The Deepening Crisis in Evangelical Christianity*. Retrieved from The Atlantic Magazine: https://www.theatlantic.com/ideas/archive/2019/07/evangelical-christians-face-deepening-crisis/593353/

Wheeler, T. (2016, June 20). *FCC Chair Tom Wheeler speaks at The National Press Club - June 20, 2016*. Retrieved from YouTube.com: https://www.youtube.com/watch?v=tNH35Kcao60

Wikipedia. (2018, March 28). *Dominionism*. Retrieved from Wikipedia: https://en.wikipedia.org/wiki/Dominion_theology

Wikipedia Contributors. (2020, February 28). *Monstrance*. Retrieved from Wikipedia: https://en.wikipedia.org/wiki/Monstrance

Wild Goose Festival. (2016, February 18). *The Wild Goose Experience.* Retrieved from YouTube: https://youtu.be/hfldkqz3nvy

Wild Olive. (2018, May 03). *United Nations.* Retrieved from Wild Olive UK: http://www.wildolive.co.uk/United%20Nations.htm

Wiles, R. (2014, July 07). *Why Did Copeland, Robison Meet With Pope Francis?* Retrieved from Charisma News: https://www.charismanews.com/opinion/44555-why-did-copeland-robison-meet-with-pope-francis

World Council of Churches. (2018, March 27). *World Council of Churches; A worldwide fellowship of churches seeking unity, a common witness and Christian service.* Retrieved from Oikoumene: https://www.oikoumene.org/en/

World Council of Churches WCC. (2018, March 27). *GETI 2018.* Retrieved from Oikoumene: https://www.oikoumene.org/en/mission2018/geti-2018

Wyatt, R. (2007, March 07). *A NOW WORD--IT'S TIME FOR THE PROPHETIC TO BE EARTHED AND THE KINGDOM OF GOD ESTABLISHED* . Retrieved from Identity Network: http://www.identitynetwork.net/apps/articles/default.asp?articleid=31188&columnid=2093

Dr. June Dawn Knight

ABOUT THE AUTHOR

We Are the Bride Ministries Founder

Dr. June Dawn Knight is an author, revivalist, media specialist, mother and grandmother. Her heart is to serve her community. She has been in public service for the last 15 years. She spearheaded four organizations. The Middle Tennessee Jr. League Cheerleader's Association in which she unified four different counties and ten cities for cheerleading. MTJLCA still exists today. She also served as the president of the Steelworker's Union for the CMCSS Bus Drivers in 2004/2005. Then, she went to World Harvest Bible College in Columbus, Ohio. Following Bible College, she attended APSU from 2008 – 2012. During her time at APSU, she spearheaded three organizations on campus. Dr. June Dawn served student life and served on the Provost Committee for the students. Please see the following newspaper articles and videos:

http://www.apsu.edu/news/new-organization-apsu-gives-voice-nontraditional-students
http://www.apsu.edu/news/4-apsu-students-establish-new- honor-society-nontraditional-students
http://www.apsu.edu/news/27-apsu-students-named-prestigious-whos-who-among-college-students
http://www.apsu.edu/news/apsu-annual-awards-program- honors-student-leaders-faculty-staff-organizations
http://www.discoverclarksville.com/articles/tag/june-dawn- knight/
http://www.youtube.com/watch?v=ZyvnE4epKDE (Video of Non-Traditional Accomplishments at APSU)
http://www.youtube.com/watch?v=tV9HKJ3PFnI (NTSS Commercial)
http://www.youtube.com/watch?v=9bjBM28lpVk (Austin's Angels TV Show)

http://www.youtube.com/watch?v=u_bOnbDZ9uI (Retirement from MTJLCA)

Dr. June Dawn graduated APSU in December 2012 with her master's Degree in Corporate Communication.

She studied in London during Grad School under the top three global Public Relations/Advertising Firms in the world. During this time under the instruction of the University of Kentucky, she made a 100 in the class. She graduated with a 3.74 GPA. Dr. June Dawn had dreams of traveling the world for a major corporation, however, after graduation, God stopped her plans and called her back to the ministry.

After submitting 100% to the call of God, she has been serving the Body of Christ in many areas such as websites for pastors, ministries, film, pictures, video, graphic designs, marketing, advertising, etc. She has used her skills to help others. Her heart is to serve the Body of Christ through the direction of the Holy Spirit. Her heart is to continue the servanthood path and help other ministers achieve their destiny as God promotes her to achieve hers. In August 2015, Dr. June Dawn Knight graduated with her Doctorate in Christian Theology at the International Miracle Institute under the direction of Dr. Christian Harfouche and Global Miracle Apostolic Faith Church.

Her Professional VITA:

Dr. June Knight is a specialist on corporate communications, social media, corporations (ministry) media, and communication implementation. Dr. June has served ministries and businesses all over the world to achieve their goals.

She partners with leaders and God to obtain the ideal outcome for the vision God placed on the inside of them. Whether it is communicating to a community, a congregation, a nation, or a certain targeted niche, Dr. June helps the visionary to articulate the vision and implement a strategy to obtain maximum effectiveness.

Dr. June's Education:
- o Bachelor's Degree in Public Relations at Austin Peay State University
- o Master's Degree in Corporate Communications at APSU One year of studies at World Harvest Bible College
- o Doctor of Theology at International Miracle Institute

While in Graduate School at APSU, Dr. June studied in London (Winter 2011/2012) and studied under the top three global marketing/advertising/communication firms in the world. She wrote a 20-page research paper comparing how the United Kingdom markets a product versus the United States. Dr. June completed the class with a grade of 100! Following graduation, Dr. June turned that paper into her first book, Mark of the Beast.

Dr. June has written eleven books. She also is the President and CEO of *We are the Bride Ministries* which includes: WATB.tv, WATB Radio. She is a TV and Radio Host and is hosting two television shows: BRIDE TIME LIVE and Clarion Call.

Dr. June traveled the entire border of the United States from March 2017 – September 2017, the Lord showed the sickness in the country. In 2018 God showed her the idols in the church and nation then sent her to Washington DC with $9 and a suitcase in 2018. She was there for a year and God did a miracle. She worked in the White House and Secretary of State department in the Press Corps. This is what led to these books.

Made in the USA
Columbia, SC
07 September 2023

22510295R00174